12 week Nutrition Programme

gavin morey

traintobecome

Myo Clinic Publishing

Copyright © 2008, 2009 & 2010

Myo Clinic Publishing

www.myoclinic.co.uk

ISBN 978-0-9564955-5-6

Acknowledgements

I don't know where to start, but I would like to thank my family and friends for all their support throughout the past five years on the making of these books. It has been a long and hard process, but it has been well worth it in the end!

I have had a lot of help from my Mum and Dad, you both mean the world to me. To my brothers, Chris, Rob and Aaron, I would like to thank you for keeping me grounded and helping me with the books and website. Thanks to my friend Simon for being there for the past 12 years with all of my silly ideas and enterprises and to Gav, for training with me and keeping me on track all the way to the end. I would also just like to say thank you to Fred for training with me throughout the 12 weeks and helping me with all of my business concerns. You have helped me more than you realise.

Finally, to my beautiful and devoted fiancée, you gave me so much help and support, especially towards the end in writing these books. Thank you and I love you so much x.

Contents

Introduction

Train to Become: 12-week Nutrition Programme is part of a three book collection dedicated to showing you how you can change your body and lifestyle in just 12 weeks.

As a personal trainer and sports therapist it is very easy for me to dictate to clients how they should live and exercise, without giving it a second thought. With this book, I provide you with the right nutritional guidance to help you to reach your potential goal for a healthier and fitter lifestyle.

I followed the step-by-step recipes throughout my 12-week programme to prove how effective and easy it can be to get healthy results. It was important to me to combat the misconceptions of dieting and 'faddy' eating plans.

There are three ways to use this book:

1. Use as a step by step guide for a daily balanced diet by selecting recipes to follow and adding them to your existing diet

2. Use as a daily food diary to keep a log of your own nutritional intake

3. Combine this book with the other books in this series – Train to Become: 12-week Fitness Programme and the Train to Become: General Health Guide and see if you can complete the 12-week challenge.

The recipes are easy to follow and have been created with a **family of four** in mind. It is important to show that following a healthy eating and balanced nutritional diet will improve you and your family's health, fitness and wellbeing. The recipe section will guide you through the number of meals that you should consume each day, when and how to prepare them and even supplies you with unique, detailed weekly shopping lists to save you time.

The shopping lists include all of the ingredients that you will need for each week's recipes and you can take a copy of the list with you when you go shopping. The lists are sectioned from carbohydrates through to meats, fish and fruit and vegetables and you will find shopping so much quicker and easier with them. Please feel free to amend the lists slightly to incorporate your existing cupboard contents.

Most recipes are suitable for vegetarians. Depending on the ingredients that you use, the recipes can also be dairy free and suitable for vegans.

Injury and disclaimer

Muscles and injuries are my field of expertise but before you begin any hard and strenuous exercise and home health testing, you should consult your GP for medical reassurance.

When I started my 12-week programme I saw my GP to explain to him what I had planned. Also I wanted to ensure that the home testing kits would give me sufficiently accurate results on which I could base my health and fitness tests.

healthy eating versus
unhealthy eating

It is never too late to make a difference and with some changes to your fitness, nutrition and lifestyle, you can make big changes, with great results.

Starting your weight loss

You may be wondering if the 12-week Nutrition Programme is going to work for you?

I know the programme works. Why? Because I did it!

Before starting this programme I went through a five month fattening up process and I put on two stone in weight. I gained weight to show exactly how to lose it by making simple changes to my diet, lifestyle and fitness.

In the five months leading up to the start of the plan I didn't exercise – even when I was working as a personal trainer. For four out of the five months, I ate unhealthily to achieve my two stone weight gain and, I will be honest, I loved getting fat at the beginning! I was able to eat an awful lot of ice cream, over-indulge on a large Christmas dinner and I didn't worry about exercising at all.

I did try to eat normally though, I would even follow families who were carrying a little excess weight around supermarkets and put into my trolley whatever they put into theirs.

For breakfast I would have cereal – the nice tasting sugary ones with semi-skimmed milk. I would snack throughout the day on crisps, chocolate and muesli bars (which by the way, are not altogether healthy as they contain large amounts of sugars and saturated fats).

I drank fizzy/sugary drinks, had two rounds of sandwiches or rolls for lunch with pre-made fillings and I ate pasta, pizzas and convenience food and indulged in a dessert after every evening meal which mainly consisted of a cake of some sort and ice cream.

I ate bread quite a lot in my weight gaining process. It is a form of food that we have become used to eating for ease in making a quick sandwich or having a piece of toast. Unfortunately bread makes us feel bloated and uncomfortable due to retaining water.

By the end of my deliberate weight gain process, I really didn't want to eat or drink anymore junk food. My body had had enough by then and the effects of my junk food diet were taking their toll on my body.

At one point I found it hard to fit into my jeans and trousers and my t-shirts ended up being a bit too snug around my midriff!

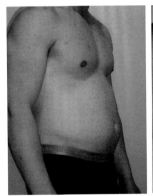

Nutrition affects 60%-70% of the way we look.

One thing I didn't like was getting spots on my face and body. I also began to get bored and frustrated with myself relaxing lazily in front of the television instead of exercising, which I quite enjoyed at first.

Thankfully, once I began to eat a healthy balanced diet, my skin cleared up, my attitude was extremely positive and my health results increased, as did my fitness results. When you get the right nutrition it contributes to around 60%–70% of how you look and feel.

If you have mistreated your body, you have the ability to change your health and wellbeing for the better, as our bodies are great at adapting to new lifestyles and diets.

With regards to the cost of my shopping bills, I was roughly spending the same amount of money eating unhealthily as I spent when I was eating healthily, give or take £5.00. You should consider that you are profiting from your health, rather than worrying about your pocket.

The best way to start this plan is by emptying the contents of your fridge and cupboards – get rid of all the junk and unhealthy foods. Not only will this give you a fresh start but it will also stop any temptations down the line!

knowing your foods

Foods come in various forms and have benefit for our bodies in different ways. We have natural foods and processed foods, but find out here why natural foods are so much more important for us.

Here is a quick rundown of every important type of food group/property that you are likely to come across:

- **Carbohydrates** – our main source of energy.
- **Proteins** – essential for growth and repair of muscle and other body tissues.
- **Fats** – a source of energy and important in relation to fat soluble vitamins.
- **Minerals** – these are inorganic elements which occur in our bodies and which are critical to its normal function.
- **Vitamins** – water and fat soluble vitamins play important roles in many chemical processes in the body.
- **Water** – is essential for our body's functions and 60%–70% of the human body is made up of it and is used to carry nutrients around, this is explained in greater detail in Train to Become Health book.

Carbohydrates (carbs)

Carbohydrate (meaning 'carbon plus water') is the most widely eaten food in the world. Along with fat and protein, carbohydrate is an essential nutrient, but what makes carbs different is that they are easily converted into energy by the body.

Carbohydrates come in two forms – simple and complex:

Simple carbohydrates – are various forms of sugar, such as glucose and sucrose (table sugar). These simple carbs have smaller molecules making it easier for them to be absorbed into the body and used as energy. Fruits, dairy products and honey contain large amounts of simple carbohydrates.

Complex carbohydrates – are composed of long string simple carbs. This means the body absorbs the large molecules at a slower rate than the simpler molecules, which gives us energy at a slower rate than simple carbs but faster than fats and protein. Complex carbs consist of rice, bread, beans and root vegetables (eg, potatoes).

Carbohydrates can also be classed as refined or unrefined:

Refined carbohydrates – means highly processed products, which strips away all of the goodness such as fibre, bran, vitamins and minerals, but still gives the same amount of calories.

The refined products are often replaced with vitamins and minerals in an unnatural way to give the food little nutritional value.

You should reduce or eliminate these types of refined products such as white bread, white rice, cakes, commercial cereals, biscuits, crisps, bagels and croissants from your diet. If you tend to get most of your carbs from these refined products you run a higher risk of getting type 2 diabetes and becoming obese.

Unrefined carbohydrates – are untouched products still retaining their own nutritional values. Brown rice, whole-grain bread, muesli and yams are all unrefined carbs.

If you consume more carbohydrates than your body needs at any one time, your body stores some of these within cells as glycogen and converts the rest into fat. So remember, only eat what you need to remain satisfied.

Protein

The body needs proteins to maintain and replace tissues and to function and grow. If the body is getting enough calories, it does not use protein for energy. If more protein is consumed than is needed, the body breaks the protein down and stores its components as fat.

Protein is the main building block in the body and is the primary component of most cells: muscle, connective tissues, hair and skin are all built from protein.

Protein consists of units called amino acids, strung together in complex formations. Because proteins are complex molecules the body takes longer to break them down. As a result, they are a much slower and a longer-lasting source of energy than carbohydrates.

Amino acids – the 20 amino acids found in proteins convey a vast array of chemical versatility. The body synthesizes some of them from components within the body, but there are nine amino acids that the body cannot synthesize. These are called essential amino acids and they must be consumed within your diet.

Essential amino acids – adults need eight of these nine amino acids: isoleucine, leucine, lysine, methioninie, phenylalanine, threonine, tryptophan, and valine. Infants also need a ninth one – histidine.

The percentage of protein the body can use to synthesize essential amino acids varies from protein to protein. The body can use 100% of the protein in an egg and a high percentage of the proteins in milk and meats.

Fats

Fats are complex molecules composed of fatty acids and glycerol. The body needs fats for growth and energy and also the body uses them to synthesize hormones and other substances (such as prostaglandins) needed for the body's activities.

Fats are the slowest source of energy but the most energy efficient form of food. Each gram of fat supplies the body with about nine calories – more than twice that supplied by proteins or carbohydrates.

By reducing the fat and sugar intake and eating healthily, the results speak for themselves – week 1 compared to week 12."

As fats are such an efficient form of energy, the body stores any excess energy as fat. The body deposits

excess fat in the abdomen (omental fat) and under the skin (subcutaneous fat) to use when it needs more energy. The body may also deposit excess fat in blood vessels and within organs, where it can block blood flow and damage organs, often causing serious disorders.

The different types of fats are:

Saturated fats – are more likely to increase cholesterol levels and increase the risk of atherosclerosis. Products containing saturated fats include: meat products (especially beef), coconut and palm oil as well as artificial hydrogenated fat.

Monounsaturated fats – normally lowers LDL cholesterol (the 'bad' cholesterol) and is found in both plant and animal products, such as olive oil, canola oil, peanut oil and in some plant foods such as avocado.

Polyunsaturated fats – tends to lower blood cholesterol levels and are found in plant sources such as safflower, sunflower, corn, cottonseed and oils like olive oils, pumpkin seeds and walnut oil.

Essential Fatty Acids (EFAs) – these are necessary fats that the human body cannot synthesise and must be obtained through diet. EFAs are long-chain polyunsaturated fatty acids derived from linolenic, linoleic, and oleic acids. There are two types of EFAs: Omega-3 and Omega-6 (Omega-9 is necessary yet 'non-essential' because the body can manufacture a modest amount on its own, provided essential EFAs are present). Essential fatty acids are found in products such as oily fish, nuts and seeds.

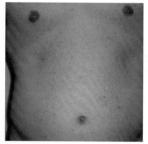 

You too can get the six pack with the right nutrition and fitness programme.

Vitamins and minerals

Vitamins and minerals make our bodies work properly and although you get vitamins and minerals from the foods you eat every day, some foods contain more vitamins and minerals than others.

Vitamins

Vitamins fall into two categories: fat soluble and water soluble.

Fat soluble – vitamins A, D, E, and K dissolve in fat and can be stored in your body. Some of these stay for a few days, some for up to six months! Then, when it's time for them to be used, your body utilises them.

Water soluble – vitamin C and the B-complex vitamins like vitamins B6, B12, niacin, riboflavin, thiamin, pantothenic acid, biotin, folic acid and folate acid, all need to dissolve in water before your body can absorb them. Because of this, your body cannot store these vitamins. Any vitamin C or B that your body does not use as it passes through your system, is lost with waste. So you need a fresh supply of these vitamins every day.

Minerals

Minerals are necessary for three main reasons:

1. Building strong bones and teeth.
2. Controlling our cells and body fluids.
3. Turning the food we eat into energy.

Whereas vitamins are organic substances (made by plants or animals), minerals are inorganic elements that come from the soil and water and are absorbed by plants or eaten by animals.

Your body needs larger amounts of some minerals, such as calcium, to grow and stay healthy. Other minerals like chromium, copper, iodine, iron, selenium and zinc are called trace minerals because you only need very small amounts of them each day.

Herbs and spices

Herbs and spices add flavour and nutrients to dishes without fat or calories. Most herbs and spices are derived from the roots, buds, bark and fruit of plants.

Herbs are usually the leaves of certain plants and have been traditionally used to treat diseases for thousands of years.

Herbs such as basil, chilli, oregano, ginger, garlic, fenugreek and rosemary are very beneficial to our health.

Many spices contain antioxidants that protect against cancer, heart disease and can even help with controlling blood sugar.

There are other spices that have properties that fight ecoli, listeria, staphylococcus and fungus. This is why most of the meals within the 12-week plan have herbs and spices within them.

Salt (sodium)

Most of our dietary salt comes from the foods we eat and other salt comes from the drinks we consume.

Both sodium and chloride are essential not only to life, but to good health – it has always been that way. The body's salt/water ratio is critical to a healthy metabolism. The human blood contains 0.9% salt (sodium chloride) and salt maintains the electrolyte balance inside and outside its cells.

Salts are found naturally in foods and drinks as well as coming in the form of sea salt, table salt, rock salt etc. There is a good side and a bad side to salt.

The bad side of salt – unnatural/processed salt has been stripped of all its goodness that sea salt provides, such as minerals.

Salt makes your body hold onto water and the extra water stored in your body raises your blood pressure. So, the more salt you eat, the higher your blood pressure.

The higher your blood pressure, the greater the risk and strain on your heart, arteries, kidneys and brain. This can lead to heart attacks, strokes, dementia and kidney disease.

The good side of salt – sea salt is actually good for you when it is natural and has not been refined. This comes directly from the sea and not only is it full of minerals but it can also enhance flavours to make our foods taste even better.

Salt is essential to our health and development. We need the vital electrolytes in salt (sodium and potassium) to control water levels in the blood and tissue.

A healthy intake of sea salt aids in balancing:

- Blood sugar levels
- The absorption of food in the intestines
- Acts as a strong and natural anti-histamine
- Can help clear mucus and phlegm from the lungs

I choose not to add any extra salt to my meals and food and I will leave it up to you whether you add salt to your meals for that extra bit of taste or not. If you do choose to use salt for seasoning, please use sea salt.

the nitty gritty

Rest assured it is very easy to follow! Whether you are going to commit to the 12-week programme or if you just want to try the recipes, they are all simple and straightforward to follow. You are not fixed to the recipes and are free to swap the meals around, even pick a different week entirely if you wish – the choice is yours!

Following the programme:

The recipes are very easy to follow and are in simple step-by-step instructions. I give you advice about when to cook tomorrow's lunch and when you should prepare a marinade for your evening meal.

On each day you will find an easy to understand nutritional diary. I used this every day to show exactly what I ate and how I managed to reach my end result. There is a diary for you to fill out too so you can monitor your progress.

Choosing the foods for you

You may be wondering when looking through the recipes, what happens if I don't like one of the key ingredients such as sweet potato or fish.

I have designed the recipes to be versatile so that you can swap and change the ingredients to suit you and your taste buds.

Major ingredient alternatives:

- Specified fruit – any fruit, not too many grapes though
- Sweet potato – potato, yam, butternut squash
- Baked potato – sweet potato, yam, butternut squash
- Fish – white meat
- Pork – beef
- Chicken – turkey

My choice of foods

When following the 12-week nutritional guide I would always choose turkey over chicken. Also, to be honest I never really consumed much skimmed milk (once every two weeks in my muesli). I would always choose rice milk/soya milk over skimmed milk.

For the following ingredients I would recommend that you use the same as I did, as they are more beneficial for the body:

- Cold pressed extra virgin olive oil
- Organic rice milk, Alpro unsweetened soya milk and skimmed milk
- Low fat bio live yoghurt
- Organic balsamic vinegar
- Jordans Natural Organic or Nut and Seed Muesli
- Make all of your own sauces and dressings
- Brown sugar
- Free range organic eggs
- Free range poultry and meat from the local butchers
- Tropicana/Innocent fruit drinks.

When to eat on training days

You should eat 1½ hours before or after exercise. Again in reality, this is just a rough timing to help as a guide. I would sometimes eat breakfast and within 40 minutes I would be cycling to work, so just listen to your body and decide what's right for you. When you finish exercise, try to eat protein within 30 minutes to fuel your muscles and help them repair. I would use soya nuts as my post exercise snack.

Time to eat

There is a lot of stipulation on what time you should eat. We all have different lifestyles and routines but sometimes it is just physically impossible to eat at a certain time. For example, I would sometimes eat later when I was working in London. All you have to remember is that you need to eat breakfast, lunch and dinner – do not worry too much about the timings. If you are eating later in the day, keep your food portions smaller than normal, increase the protein and decrease your carbohydrate intake.

Bad day? Bad week?
Don't panic!

This is not an eating plan that denies you any naughty foods or treats. I still had the odd off-day! When you do get a bad day, sit back for a moment, analyse what you are doing and ask yourself:

1. Are you eating for the sake of eating?

2. Are you eating because you're hungry?

3. Have your treat foods got out of hand?

4. Are you depriving yourself from snacks/treats?

5. Are you missing meals?

6. Are you drinking enough water?

7. Are you eating or drinking more sugary foods than normal?

Just ask why are you having your bad day and perhaps you will stop and think before you reach for the bad food.

If you do have a bad day or an entire week – try not to panic. Limit these days as much as possible but remember this: don't give up! If you hang in there and turn your food back around to being good, you can actually lose more weight than you have possibly put on with your bad food. Your body will get a shock and like always it will adapt to its current circumstances.

If you find this hard to believe look at the Train to Become Health Guide and Female Fitness Programme books:

Week 5 fat % – 28.4
Week 6 fat % – 27.4
Week 7 Fat % – 28.4
Week 8 Fat % – 26.3
Week 12 Fat % – 21.3

You will notice that during week 7, the weight started to creep up due to a series of bad days, OK, a bad week! From week eight, in just five weeks she managed to lose 7.1% body fat, just by turning around the way she was eating!

Week 5, Week 8 and Week 12. There is a noticeable change around the midriff, especially in the last four weeks.

This was due to having too many treat foods and starting to have a taste for sugar. I analysed what was being eaten by the female and then counteracted it by following the nutritional program precisely, with sensible snacks just like the ones listed later in this chapter.

Eating out

Don't panic if you're going to eat out. Look at it as a treat that you deserve from time to time, but of course that doesn't mean run wild and eat what you want! I ate out on average once every three weeks and all you need to remember is the basics of food.

Perhaps lean towards more fish or protein dishes with less sauce, fresh food and not so many starchy carbohydrates.

Foods to avoid when eating out:

• Creamy dishes

• Starchy carbohydrates

• Deep fried food

• Pan fried food

• Battered food

• Bread

• Chips

• Desserts

Do not be afraid to state how you want your food cooked when ordering. For instance, you may ask for a jacket potato instead of chips or dressing on the side rather than over your meal. If you do need something sweet after dinner go for fresh fruit or if you find that too boring, share a dessert with someone!

To take away
or not to take away?

Truthfully, I didn't have a take-away for years. This is mainly due to the fact that I would rather eat out or cook. If I cooked, I found that at least I would know what was in my food – no added sugars, preservatives and so on. I recommend that you try to stay clear of take-aways and convenience foods if you can.

Food portions and presentation

Within each recipe and shopping list, I have given you all the requirements that you will need for breakfast, lunch and dinner. This is a guideline though as sometimes, for example, during the week, I would eat two turkey breasts instead of the one recommended. Also, I recommend eating 60g of muesli but that was not enough for me, so I ended up eating roughly 100g for breakfast to give me the energy for the day ahead.

Surprisingly, the presentation of your food is almost as important as how it tastes! It has been proven that good food presentation can actually make your food taste even better due to your brain perceiving that the food looks delicious and smells delectable before even tasting it. So take your time with all your meal presentations.

Shopping lists

The shopping lists are listed in alphabetical order under categories of fish, meat, dairy, carbohydrates, fruit, vegetables, herbs and spices and other. This will help you be in and out of the supermarkets with so much more ease and efficiency. All the lists have been designed to cover every meal, but you do need to add your healthy snacks to your list.

When you start, you will notice that the amounts are very precise but these are just recommendations. For instance, if you cannot find 12 cherry tomatoes, only a pack of eight, don't worry because the recipes are adaptable.

As you can see, the shopping lists are fairly adaptable as are the recipes. If, for example, you don't like to eat sweet potatoes or butternut squash you can eat yam instead. If like me, you would rather eat turkey instead of chicken because it is leaner and healthier, you can! You are the boss, just be good to yourself.

It is important when you are shopping to not worry so much about the calories, but look carefully at the carbohydrates (sugars), and the fats (saturated) that you are popping into your supermarket trolley.

Treat foods

You will notice that from time to time I would have foods that would be classed as bad foods or 'treat foods'.

Think of it this way – you are not a robot and you are not on a diet – you are on a healthy eating plan! This 12-week Nutrition Plan consists of 80% – 90 % healthy eating with the rest being considered naughty.

The treat days will act as motivation too and help keep you on track to your potential end goal. If however, you are the sort of person who cannot just have a little treat, you have to finish the entire tub of ice cream – then resist and don't have any treats at all! You know your body; just don't starve it from the nutrients it needs.

I suggest that you don't buy treats on your main shopping trips and don't leave them out on display. You won't be so tempted to eat them if they're sitting in the cupboard!

Desserts and snacks

During the 12-week Programme I had two healthy desserts a week which would normally be yoghurt and fruit, fruit salad with seeds or just a fruit salad. However, for the first two weeks of the programme, I had no desserts at all and kept to the recipes exactly.

Snacks are just that, snacks. They are not mini meals, so don't treat them as such. I would never purchase snacks that are high in sugar or fat (carbohydrate sugar over 5g or saturated fat over 5g). Surprisingly, this counts out all of the cereal bars on offer at your local supermarket. Try to stay clear of them as these bars will tend you to give you a sugar craving, which in turn makes you hungry.

Listed below is what I would eat as snacks and the average of how much I ate per week.

Snack List

- **Fruits:**

  Melon, mango or coconut – 1 to share

  Peach, plum, or kiwi – 1

  Pineapple – 1 to share (I had 2 slices a week)

  Orange or nectarine – 1

  Berries (blackberries, goji, blueberries, raspberries or strawberries) – 2 portions

  Pear – 1

  Banana – 5

  Apple – 5

- **Dr Karg crackers** – 3
- **Crackers/flat breads** – 1
- **Small bowl of muesli** (if really hungry) – 2
- **Yoghurt/soya yoghurt** (four dessert spoons) – 1
- **Nuts** (cashew, pine or occasionally mixed nuts) – 2 to 3 handfuls
- **Soya nuts** – after all training sessions 3 to 4 handfuls
- **Seeds** (pumpkin or sunflower) – 2 to 3 handfuls
- **Pitta bread/wrap with salad and protein filling** – 1

I would roughly snack four to five times a day at random intervals. On average however, I snacked at 10.00am, 12.00pm, 2.30pm and 4.00pm. You can use this as a guide, but you do not need to snack five times a day – just when you need to.

A word about fruit drinks

The main point to remember when choosing a fruit juice drink is to buy one that is not made from concentrates and is 100% natural, with no added sweeteners or preservatives.

Frequently asked questions:

Will I get bored with the 12-week Nutrition Plan?

The recipes have been created so that you don't eat the same meals each week and you have a different dinner recipe every day for the whole 12 weeks. With this wide variety and varied cooking, your taste buds should not be feeling neglected.

Will I be able to feed the whole family?

This is a plan based around a family of four.

Will I get hungry?

To be honest, there will be times when you will feel hungrier than usual, but there will be days where you feel full. When you first start the programme, your body and eating habits will change so you will probably find that the first two weeks are the most demanding. The 12-week Nutrition Plan has been particularly devised to fulfil your appetite with tantalizing meals that will keep hunger at bay.

Remember if you are following the Train to Become Fitness and Health books as well, you may require more food for different days than others. Follow the plan and use my diary as a guide and you should end up getting where you want to be – good luck.

Is the shopping list easy to follow?

The shopping list has been designed to fall into categories as well as to be in alphabetical order. This will enable you to shop more quickly and easily.

How easy is it to follow the nutrition book along side the fitness book and health book?

It is very easy, I followed all three books together to make sure this was achievable and it was. If you do follow all three books together and success, you will have completed the Train to Become Challenge!

Did you use supplements?

No. This is mainly to show that if you are on the right healthy eating plan, then you don't need any supplements. I am not against supplements as some of them are beneficial for the body.

Food measurements and conversions

Measuring liquids

Teaspoon (tsp)	Tablespoon (tbsp)	Fluid Ounce (oz)
3	1	½
6	2	1
48	16	8

Cups (8oz)	Glass (8oz)	Pints	Millilitres (ml)
1	1	½	237 ml
2	2	1	474 ml
4	4	2	946ml/0.9 litres
8	8	4	1892ml/1.9 litres

Measuring solids

Tablespoon (tbsp)	Ounces (fluid)	Cups (8oz)	Grams (g) actual		Pounds (lbs)
1	½	$1/16$	15	(14.3)	-
2	1	$1/8$	25	(28.3)	-
4	2	¼	50	(56.7)	-
8	4	½	100	(114.3)	¼
16	8	1	225	(228.6)	½
32	16	2	450	(457.1)	1
48	24	3	700	(685.7)	1½
64	32	4	900	(914.3)	2

Oven temperature

Centigrade (C)	Fahrenheit (F)	Gas Mark
80	175	-
90	190	-
100	200	-
110	225	¼
130	250	½
140	275	1
150	300	2
170	325	3
180	350	4
190	375	5
200	400	6
220	425	7
230	450	8
240	475	9

Quick conversions

3 teaspoon = 1 tablespoon

2 tablespoons = 1 fluid oz

8 tablespoons = ½ cup

16 tablespoons = 1 cup

1 cup/glass = 8 fluid oz/100 grams

2 cups = 1 pint

16 oz = 1 pound

4½ cups liquid = 1 pound

1 kilogram = 2.2 pounds

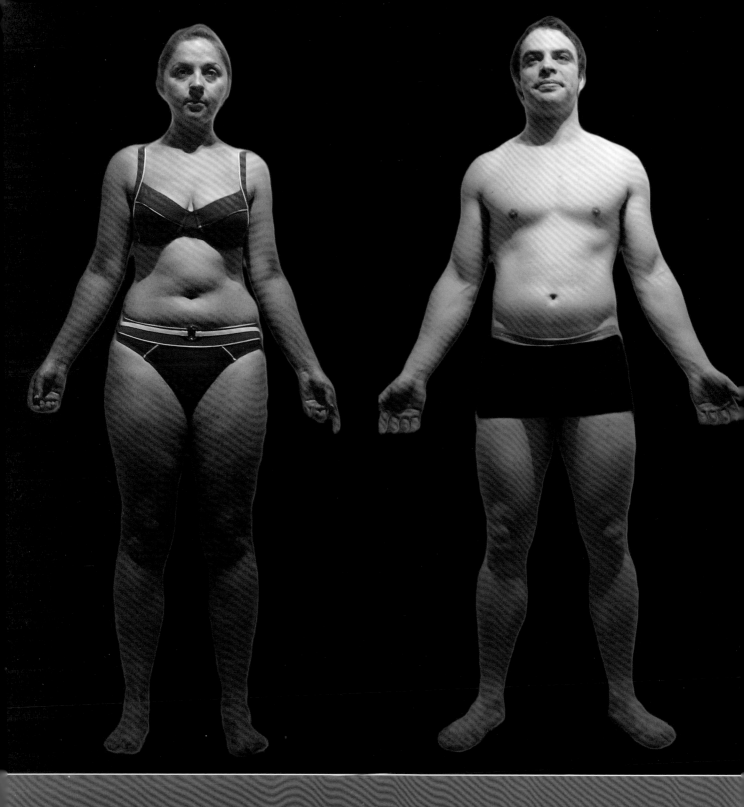

enjoy your food
week 1

Week 1 Overview

DAY	BREAKFAST	LUNCH	DINNER
1	Muesli with fresh fruit	Smoked salmon pitta bread	Beef stir fry
2	Fruit porridge	Tuna and olive salad	Chicken with roasted sweet potatoes
3	Fresh fruit and seeds	Tuna salad with sweet potato	Slow roasted orange veal
4	Wheat biscuits/Shredded Wheat or muesli with fruit	Turkey wrap	Jacket potatoes with cheese
5	Fruit salad	Butternut squash and vegetables	Spicy salmon
6	Smoothie	Tuna and olive salad	Grilled tandoori chicken
7	Omelette	Butternut squash and coriander soup	Mackerel salad

Snack list

- **Fruits:**

    Melon, mango or coconut – 1 to share

    Peach, plum, or kiwi – 1

    Pineapple – 1 to share (I had 2 slices a week)

    Orange or nectarine – 1

    Berries (blackberries, goji, blueberries, raspberries or strawberries) – 2 portions

    Pear – 1

    Banana – 5

    Apple – 5

- **Dr Karg crackers** – 3

- **Crackers/flat breads** – 1

- **Small bowl of muesli** (if really hungry) – 2

- **Yoghurt/soya yoghurt** (four dessert spoons) – 1

- **Nuts** (cashew, pine or occasionally mixed nuts) – 2 to 3 handfuls

- **Soya nuts** – after all training sessions 3 to 4 handfuls

- **Seeds** (pumpkin or sunflower) – 2 to 3 handfuls

- **Pitta bread/wrap with salad and protein filling** – 1

I would roughly snack four to five times a day at random intervals. On average however, I snacked at 10.00am, 12.00pm, 2.30pm and 4.00pm. You can use this as a guide, but you do not need to snack five times a day – just when you need to.

Shopping List
Week 1

Carbohydrates:

1 bag of brown rice
480g of Jordans muesli
1 bag of pine nuts
8 wholemeal/brown pitta breads
240g porridge oats
4 jacket potatoes
1 bag of sunflower seeds
1 bag of pumpkin seeds
9 sweet potatoes
4 organic tortilla wraps
Wheat biscuits/Shredded wheat

Dairy and non-dairy alternatives:

350g mature cheddar/goat's
    hard cheese
8 eggs
40g feta/goat's cheese
1 light soft cheese /
    soft goat's cheese
680ml skimmed/Alpro soya/rice
    /oat milk
2kg Alpro soya/plain yoghurt

Fish:

8 anchovy fillets
4 mackerel fillets
4 salmon fillets
1 pack of smoked salmon
4 small tuna cans
350g tuna steaks

Meat:

4 200g beef steaks
8 chicken breasts
400g lean ham
8 turkey breasts
1.4kg rack of veal

Fruit:

6 apples
12 bananas
1 punnet of blueberries
2 lemons
2 mangos
1 orange
1 large pineapple
1 punnet of raspberries

Vegetables:

1 avocado
100g baby corn
2 bags of baby spinach
25g black olives
3 butternut squash
5 carrots
2 celery sticks
2 courgettes
1 cucumber
175g french beans
2 leeks
4 lettuces
265g mange tout
150g mushrooms
1 onion
115g plum tomatoes
5 red onions
5 red peppers
20 red tomatoes
100g rocket salad
26 spring onions
1 bag of sweet corn
2 yellow peppers

Herbs:

Basil
Black pepper
Chinese five spice
Coriander
Cumin
Dill
Fresh ginger
1 garlic clove
Green chilli
Ground coriander
Mint
Nutmeg
Paprika
Turmeric

Other:

Balsamic vinegar
Chicken stock
Cold pressed extra virgin olive oil
Ginger wine
Soy sauce
Tandoori paste
Tomato puree

Snacks:

Fruit
Dr Karg crackers/flat breads
Small bowl of muesli
Alpro soya yoghurt
Nuts (cashew, pine or
    occasionally mixed nuts)
Soya nuts
Seeds (pumpkin or sunflower)

Fruit drinks

1 carton Tropicana/Innocent fruit
drink

Recipes for Week 1: Day 1

Meal   Time Description
Breakfast:

Snacks:

Lunch:

Snacks:

Dinner:

Snacks:

Muesli with fruit

240g muesli (60g per person)
Serving of milk (soya/rice/oat or skimmed milk)
Fruit of your choice, cut into chunks (1 piece of fruit per person)

1. Pour muesli into a bowl, add milk.
2. Serve with fruit.

Smoked salmon pitta

4 wholemeal pitta breads (hot or cold)
Smoked salmon
Soft goat's/low fat soft cheese
(small serving per person)

2 spring onions, finely sliced
200g baby spinach
4 large tomatoes, sliced into quarters
1 red pepper, finely sliced

1. Cut open the pitta bread and spread the goat's cheese thinly across one side.
2. Add the smoke salmon and sprinkle the spring onions.
3. Serve with spinach, tomatoes and red pepper.

Beef stir fry

2 teaspoons corn flour
115ml beef stock
2 tablespoons soy sauce
800g of lean steak
1 tablespoon olive oil
1 garlic clove, finely chopped

2cm piece ginger
150g mushrooms
4 spring onions, chopped
100g of mange-tout
Serve with brown rice

1. Blend together the stock, corn flour and soy sauce.
2. Mix the beef, olive oil, garlic and ginger in a large bowl.
3. Heat a large frying pan or wok and when hot, add beef mixture and heat until meat is brown, set aside.
4. Add the spring onions, mange-tout and mushrooms to the hot pan and fry until slightly crunchy.
5. Add the stock and corn flour mixture to the pan, stir over high heat until sauce has thickened.
6. Replace the meat back into the pan, heat and stir well, serve with brown rice.

Recipes for Week 1: Day 2

BREAKFAST

Fruit porridge

240g of porridge oats (60g per person)
2-3 apples, chopped
120ml of water or milk (soya/rice/oat or skimmed milk) –
enough to cover the oats and apples

1. Slowly bring to the boil the water and/or milk in a sauce pan. Add the oats and chopped apples.
2. Cook for 10 minutes, stirring continuously until thickened. If the mixture becomes too thick, add more water or milk. Serve immediately.

LUNCH

Tuna and olive salad

175g french beans, topped and tailed
350g fresh tuna steaks
115g baby plum tomatoes, halved
8 anchovy fillets, drained on kitchen paper
25g stoned black olives in brine, drained
Fresh basil leaves to garnish

For the dressing:
1 tablespoon olive oil
1 garlic clove, crushed
1 tablespoon lemon juice
1 tablespoon basil leaves, shredded

1. Boil the french beans in a small saucepan for 5 minutes, or until slightly tender, drain and keep warm.
2. Season the tuna steaks with black pepper and place tuna on grill rack and cook for 4–5 minutes on each side, or until cooked through.
3. Drain the tuna on kitchen paper and using a knife and fork, flake the tuna into bite size pieces.
4. Mix the tuna, french beans, tomatoes, anchovies and olives into a bowl and keep warm.
5. Mix all of the dressing ingredients together and pour over tuna salad and garnish with basil and serve.

DINNER

Chicken with roasted sweet potatoes

3 sweet potatoes, chopped
1 butternut squash, peeled and chopped
1 red onion, peeled and chopped
6 spring onions, finely sliced
40g feta/goat's cheese, cut into small chunks

4 chicken breasts, sliced
2 tablespoon olive oil
1 teaspoon dried basil
3 tomatoes, roughly chopped
Handful of lettuce per person

1. Preheat oven 190°C (375°F). Place the sweet potatoes and butternut squash into an ovenproof dish and drizzle half of the extra virgin olive oil over the top, mix well. Place into the oven and cook for 35–45 minutes.
2. Meanwhile, heat the rest of the extra virgin olive oil over medium heat and cook the chicken breasts for 8–12 minutes or until golden brown and thoroughly cooked.
3. Add the red onion and spring onions, dried basil and tomatoes to the sweet potatoes and butternut squash dish, stir well and cook for a further 5 minutes.
4. Sprinkle the cheese over the top and cook for another 3–4 minutes.
5. Serve the sweet potatoes and butternut squash topped with cheese with the chicken on a bed of lettuce leaves. Decorate with spring onions.

PREPARE

Lunch for tomorrow: Tuna salad with sweet potato

1. Preheat oven to 190°C (375°F). Cut sweet potatoes into small chunks and drizzle a tablespoon of exra virgin olive oil. Place into oven for 30–40 minutes.
2. Once cooked and cooled, place into the fridge ready for tomorrow's lunch.

Recipes for Week 1: Day 3

BREAKFAST

Fresh fruit and seeds

8 tablespoons soya/plain yoghurt
Sprinkle of sunflower or pumpkin seeds
2 pieces of fruit of your choice per person

1. Mix together the soya/plain yoghurt, seeds and fruit
2. Divide into 4 portions.

LUNCH

Tuna salad with sweet potato

4 sweet potatoes, cooked (1 per person)
4 small tinned tuna, (1 per person)
100g rocket leaves
4 tomatoes, roughly chopped
¼ cucumber, roughly chopped

50g mange-tout
1 red pepper, sliced
1 tablespoon balsamic vinegar
1 tablespoon olive oil

1. Preheat oven 190°C (375°F).
2. Cut the sweet potatoes into small chunks and drizzle a tablespoon of extra virgin olive oil and cook in the oven for 30–40 minutes.
3. Place rocket leaves, mange-tout, tomatoes, cucumber and red pepper into a salad bowl.
4. Add balsamic vinegar and olive oil and mix well.
5. Serve with tuna, sweet potatoes and salad.

DINNER

Slow roasted orange veal

1.4kg rack of veal, trim fat
1 butternut squash, peeled and chopped into small pieces
2 carrots, sliced lengthways
2 courgettes, chopped
2 red onions, chopped
2 tablespoons olive oil
4 spring onions, finely chopped
Orange zest, finely grated
60ml of orange juice

For the dressing:
150g low fat natural/soya yoghurt
2 tablespoons fresh mint
½ tablespoon olive oil
2 tablespoons lemon juice

1. Preheat oven 200°C (400°F). Put butternut squash, carrots, courgettes and onions into a large baking dish. Drizzle over half of the olive oil and mix well.
2. Mix the spring onions, orange zest, orange juice and the rest of the olive oil to make a mixture.
3. Place veal on a wire rack set over vegetables and coat meat with mixture.
4. Roast veal for 40 minutes or until cooked throughout.
5. Remove meat from oven, cover with foil and rest for 10 minutes.
6. Mix all of the dressing ingredients into a bowl and serve vegetables and meat with a drizzle of dressing over the top.

PREPARE

Lunch for tomorrow: Turkey wrap

1. Heat some extra virgin olive oil (½ tablespoon) in a frying pan over a medium heat.
2. Slice and cook until golden, 4 turkey breasts (1 per person).

Recipes for Week 1: Day 4

BREAKFAST

Wheat biscuits, Shredded Wheat or muesli with a fruit

560ml milk (soya/rice/oat or skimmed milk)
2-3 wheat biscuits/Shredded Wheat or 240g of muesli, (60g per person)
1 piece of fruit of your choice

1. Place your choice of cereal in a bowl add milk.
2. Serve with fruit.

LUNCH

Turkey wrap

4 turkey breasts, cooked and sliced
4 organic wholewheat wraps, serve hot or cold
200g mixed salad
4-5 tomatoes, sliced

1 red onion, finely chopped
1 yellow pepper, sliced
4 tablespoons of soya/plain yoghurt

1. Place the salad, red onion, tomatoes, yellow pepper and cooked turkey breasts into a salad bowl and mix well.
2. Drizzle over the yoghurt and add the salad to the wrap and roll up.

DINNER

Jacket potatoes with cottage or goat's cheese

4 large baking potatoes (cut a cross in the centre of each potato and prick the skins with a fork)
3 teaspoons sun-dried tomato puree
½ teaspoon ground coriander
1 tablespoon olive oil
4 spring onions, finely chopped
1 fresh green chilli, deseeded and finely chopped
1 tablespoon fresh coriander

350g low fat cottage cheese/soft goat's cheese
Handful of pine nuts

Side salad:
Generous amounts of mixed salad leaves
4 large tomatoes, chopped
1 red pepper, chopped
¼ cucumber, chopped

1. Preheat oven to 200°C (400°F). Bake the potatoes for one hour or until soft and cooked. Meanwhile prepare the salad.
2. Mix the sun-dried tomato puree and ground coriander together in a bowl.
3. Just before the potatoes are ready, heat the olive oil in a small saucepan and add the spring onions and chopped chillies and cook for 2–3 minutes, stirring occasionally until soft.
4. Stir in the sun-dried tomato paste and cook for a further 1 minute. Remove from heat and stir in the chopped coriander.
5. Place the cheese in a bowl and stir in the tomato mixture.
6. Divide the cheese mixture equally among the potatoes.
7. Serve with salad and add a sprinkle of pine nuts over the top.

PREPARE

Lunch for tomorrow: Butternut squash and vegetables

1. Preheat the oven to 190°C (375°F). Place the butternut squash, sweet potatoes onion and leek into a large baking dish. Drizzle with olive oil and season with pepper and coriander.
2. Cook for 30–40 minutes or until vegetables are cooked, stir if necessary.
3. Meanwhile, place all of the dressing ingredients into a small bowl and gently mix.
4. Serve with dressing drizzled over the top.

Your food diary:

Meal   Time   Description

Breakfast:

Snacks:

Lunch:

Snacks:

Dinner:

Snacks:

Recipes for Week 1: Day 5

BREAKFAST

Fruit salad

8 tablespoons soya/plain yoghurt (2 tablespoons per person)

80g oats

60g sunflower seeds or pumpkin seeds

4-5 pieces of fruit (preferably ones in season)

1. Dice fruit into chunks and divide into 4 portions.
2. Add 2 tablespoons of soya/plain yoghurt to each portion and sprinkle with oats and seeds.

LUNCH

Butternut squash and vegetables

1 butternut squash, peeled and chopped

2 sweet potatoes, peeled, and diced into cubes

1 leek, chopped

1 red onion, quartered

1 tablespoon, olive oil

Coriander, Handful of chopped

Handful of rocket leaves per person

For the dressing:

¼ grated cucumber

4 tablespoons soya/plain yogurt

1 tablespoon olive oil

1 teaspoon balsamic vinegar

2 teaspoons black pepper

2 teaspoons dried dill

1. Preheat the oven to 190°C (375°F). Place the butternut squash, sweet potatoes, with the onion and leek into a large baking dish. Drizzle with olive oil and season with black pepper and coriander.
2. Cook for 30–40 minutes, or until vegetables are cooked, stir if necessary.
3. Meanwhile, place all dressing ingredients into a small bowl and mix well.
4. Remove from the oven and serve with rocket leaves and drizzle the dressing over the top

DINNER

Spicy salmon

4 Salmon fillets

2 teaspoons Chinese 5 Spice powder

2.5cm ginger, cut into thin strips

2 tablespoons ginger wine

2 tablespoons soy sauce

1 tablespoon olive oil

Side vegetables:

1 leek, finely shredded

1 carrot, sliced lengthways

115g mange-tout, cut into thin strips

Serve with brown rice

1. Rub Chinese five spice powder into both sides of the salmon fillets.
2. Place vegetables into a bowl, and add ginger wine and soy sauce.
3. Preheat the grill to medium heat. Boil water and add the rice.
4. Place the salmon fillets on the grill and brush with some soy sauce and cook for a few minutes each side.
5. Meanwhile, heat olive oil in wok or frying pan and stir fry vegetables for 3–5 minutes.
6. When the vegetables and salmon are cooked, transfer to plates and serve with brown rice.

PREPARE

Marinade for tomorrow's dinner: Grilled tandoori chicken

1 tablespoon tandoori paste

1 teaspoon cumin

1 garlic clove, crushed

300g natural soya/plain yoghurt

1 tablespoon lemon juice

1. In a bowl gently mix together the tandoori paste, cumin, lemon juice and yoghurt, along with the garlic.
2. Dice the chicken and coat in the marinade to leave in fridge overnight.

Your food diary:

Meal   Time   Description

Breakfast:

Snacks:

Lunch:

Snacks:

Dinner:

Snacks:

Recipes for Week 1: Day 6

BREAKFAST

Fruit smoothie

2 large mangos, peeled and chopped
4 bananas, chopped
2 handfuls of raspberries

Blend mangos, bananas and raspberries and serve.

LUNCH

Pitta turkey salad

4 wholemeal pitta breads
4 turkey breasts, cooked and sliced
Generous amount of salad leaves
1 avocado, sliced
1 red pepper, sliced

1 yellow pepper, sliced
2 spring onions, finely chopped
½ tablespoon olive oil
4 tablespoons of soya/plain yoghurt

1. Place the salad leaves, avocado, peppers and chopped spring onions in a salad bowl and mix.
2. Slice open the pitta bread and fill with turkey, salad and add a dollop of soya/plain yoghurt.
3. Serve immediately

DINNER

Grilled tandoori chicken

100g natural soya/plain yoghurt
4 chicken breasts, diced
300g spinach
1 handful of coriander, chopped
8–10 tablespoons of sweet corn
Serve with brown rice

For the marinade:
1 tablespoon tandoori paste
1 teaspoon cumin
300g natural soya/plain yoghurt
1 tablespoon lemon juice
1 garlic glove, crushed

1. In a bowl, add the marinade ingredients together and mix well.
2. Add the diced chicken and coat with marinade. Leave in the fridge for at least 2–3 hours.
3. Preheat grill to a medium heat and cover a baking tray with baking paper.
4. Skewer the chicken and place onto a baking tray. Grill for 8–12 minutes or until chicken is cooked and keep turning.
5. Boil the rice and add the sweet corn to the rice for the last 2 minutes.
6. Serve the chicken, spinach, sweet corn and rice. Pour the remaining yoghurt over the top and garnish with coriander.

NOTES

Recipes for Week 1: Day 7

Your food diary:

Meal   Time   Description

Breakfast:

Snacks:

Lunch:

Snacks:

Dinner:

Snacks:

Omelette

8 eggs (2 eggs per person)
4 tablespoons of cold water
8 teaspoons of extra virgin olive oil cold pressed
400g lean ham
1 courgette, finely sliced
4 spring onions, finely chopped

1. Cook one omelette at a time, beat the eggs with some water in a bowl.
2. Heat the extra virgin olive oil in a non stick pan over a high heat and pour in the eggs. Cook for 2 minutes or until the mixture just begins to set.
3. Place ham and courgette on top of the egg mixture and cook until the omelette has set.
4. Sprinkle on the spring onions, fold omelette in half and serve.

Butternut squash and coriander soup

900ml of chicken stock
1kg butternut squash, peeled and chopped
1 onion, roughly chopped
2 carrots, roughly chopped
2 celery sticks, roughly chopped

1 garlic clove, crushed
1 teaspoon paprika
½ teaspoon turmeric
½ teaspoon ground coriander
½ teaspoon ground nutmeg

1. In a large saucepan bring chicken stock to the boil, add the vegetables and spices and bring back to the boil.
2. Reduce heat and simmer for 20 minutes, or until vegetables are soft.
3. Allow to cool and serve.

Mackerel salad

4 cooked mackerel, remove skin
Generous amount of mixed salad leaves
1 red pepper, sliced and deseeded
4–5 tomatoes, sliced
¼ cucumber, sliced

For the dressing:
3 tablespoons of soya/plain yoghurt
Pine nuts, small sprinkle
½ tablespoon balsamic vinegar
Black pepper

1. Place mixed salad leaves, peppers, tomatoes and cucumber on a plate.
2. Cut the mackerel into pieces and place on top of salad.
3. To make the dressing, mix the yoghurt, pine nuts, balsamic vinegar in a small bowl and add black pepper to taste. Add dressing to salad.

Lunch for tomorrow: Beetroot salad

1. Preheat oven to 200°C (400°F). Place brown and wild rice in a medium sauce pan of water and bring to boil. Simmer for 20–30 minutes.
2. Place shallots on a baking tray, drizzle with olive oil and roast for 8–10 minutes.
3. Drain rice and allow to cool and refrigerate. Mix in the other ingredients the next day.

enjoy your food
week 2

Week 2 Overview

DAY	BREAKFAST	LUNCH	DINNER
1	Fruit salad	Beetroot salad	Lamb ratatouille
2	Muesli with fresh fruit	Lamb with feta/goat's cheese	Chilli fish
3	Scrambled egg with wild mushrooms	Tuna salad with sweet potato	Turkey stir fry with orange
4	Fruit porridge	Vegetable soup	Tuna steak and cannellini bean salad
5	Fresh fruit and seeds	Beef salad pitta	Tandoori turkey salad
6	Fruit smoothie	Bean salad	Swordfish with mediterranean vegetables
7	Omelette	Tuna and olive salad	Hot bean soup with butternut squash

Snack list

- **Fruits:**

  Melon, mango or coconut – 1 to share

  Peach, plum, or kiwi – 1

  Pineapple – 1 to share (I had 2 slices in a week)

  Orange or nectarine – 1

  Berries (blackberries, goji, blueberries, raspberries or strawberries) – 2 portions

  Pear – 1

  Banana – 5

  Apple – 5

- **Dr Karg crackers** – 3

- **Crackers/flat breads** – 1

- **Small bowl of muesli** (if really hungry) – 2

- **Yoghurt/soya yoghurt** (four dessert spoons) – 1

- **Nuts** (cashew, pine or occasionally mixed nuts) – 2 to 3 handfuls

- **Soya nuts** – after all training sessions 3 to 4 handfuls

- **Seeds** (pumpkin or sunflower) – 2 to 3 handfuls

- **Pitta bread/wrap with salad and protein filling** – 1

I would roughly snack four to five times a day at random intervals. On average however, I snacked at 10.00am, 12.00pm, 2.30pm and 4.00pm. You can use this as a guide, but you do not need to snack five times a day – just when you need to.

Shopping List

Week 2

Carbohydrates:

1 bag of brown rice
75g butternut beans
400g cannellini beans
50g tinned chickpeas
250g couscous
475g kidney beans
490g Jordans muesli
10 new potatoes
1 bag of pine nuts
400g pinto beans
8 wholemeal or brown
  pitta breads
320g porridge oats
1 bag of sunflower seeds
1 bag of pumpkin seeds
8 sweet potatoes
4 bags of wild rice
Wheat biscuits/Shredded wheat

Dairy and non-dairy alternatives:

20 eggs
40g feta/goat's cheese
1520ml skimmed/Alpro soya/rice
  /oat milk
2kg Alpro soya yoghurt

Fish:

8 anchovy fillets
4 plaice fillets
4 salmon fillets
1 pack of smoked salmon
200g (x 4) swordfish
4 small tuna cans
750g tuna steaks

Meat:

400g cooked roast beef
6 lamb chops
400g lean ham
8 turkey breasts
1.4kg rack of veal

Fruit:

7 apples
2 apricots
6 bananas
1 punnet of blueberries
2 lemons
1 lime
1 orange
2 peaches
1 large pineapple
1 punnet of raspberries

Vegetables:

2 avocados
4 baby aubergines
2 bags of baby spinach
4 cooked beetroot
25g black olives
175g broccoli
250g cherry tomatoes
1 butternut squash
6 carrots
4 celery sticks
5 courgettes
1 cucumber
175g french beans
2 leeks
3 lettuces
50g mange tout
8 mushrooms
5 onions
135g plum tomatoes
8 red onions
3 red peppers
10 red tomatoes
100g rocket salad
8 spring onions
4 shallots
1 bag of sweet corn
1 yellow pepper

Fruit drinks

1 carton Tropicana/Innocent fruit
drink

Herbs:

Basil
Black pepper
Cayenne pepper
Chilli powder
Chinese five spice
Chives
Coriander
Cumin
Fresh ginger
Garam masala
1 garlic clove
Ground coriander
Ground pepper
Mint
Parsley
1 red chilli
Rosemary
Turmeric

Other:

Balsamic vinegar
Chicken stock
Chilli sauce
Cold pressed extra virgin olive oil
Corn flour
Dijon mustard
Ginger wine
Soy sauce
Sesame oil
Tandoori paste
400g tinned tomatoes
Tomato puree
Vegetable stock
White wine vinegar
Wholegrain mustard

Snacks:

Fruit
Dr Karg Crackers
Crackers/flat breads
Small bowl of muesli
Yoghurt/Alpro soya yoghurt
Nuts (cashew, pine or
  occasionally mixed nuts)
Soya nuts
Seeds (pumpkin or sunflower)

Recipes for Week 2: Day 1

Your food diary:

Meal	Time	Description
Breakfast:		
Snacks:		
Lunch:		
Snacks:		
Dinner:		
Snacks:		

Fruit salad

8 tablespoons soya/plain yoghurt (2 tablespoons per person)

80g oats

60g sunflower seeds or pumpkin seeds

4–5 pieces of fruit (preferably ones in season)

1. Dice fruit into chunks and divide into 4 portions.
2. Add 2 tablespoons of soya/plain yoghurt in each portion and sprinkle with oats and seeds.

Beetroot salad

100g brown rice

100g wild rice

4 shallots, peeled and halved

2 teaspoons olive oil

4 beetroot, finely diced cooked

Juice of 1 lemon

2 tablespoons fresh mint, chopped

2 tablespoons fresh chives, chopped

1. Preheat oven to 200°C (400°F). Place brown/wild rice in medium sauce pan of water, bring to boil and simmer for 20–30 minutes.
2. Put the shallots on a baking tray, drizzle with olive oil and roast for 8–10 minutes.
3. Drain the rice and allow to cool. Gently mix together the beetroot, lemon juice and mint.
4. Stir in shallots and chives and serve.

Lamb ratatouille

8 lamb steaks, lean diced

1 tablespoon olive oil

250g couscous

Spices

1 tablespoon pepper, freshly ground

2 teaspoons coriander seeds, whole

1 teaspoon garam masala

1 teaspoon chilli powder

For the ratatouille:

2 teaspoons olive oil

4 baby aubergines

1 onion, finely chopped

1 clove garlic, chopped

1 red pepper, deseeded and sliced

1 courgette, sliced

115ml chicken stock

2 tomatoes

1 tablespoon parsley, chopped

1. Mix all the spices in a bowl and brush the steaks with a little olive oil and coat with spice mixture, cover with cling film and refrigerate for 1 hour.
2. To make ratatouille, heat the olive oil in a large frying pan over medium heat.
3. Add aubergines and cook for 4 minutes or until golden. Then add the onion and garlic and cook until lightly coloured.
4. Next add the red pepper and courgette and cook for a further minute. Then pour on the chicken stock and add the tomatoes and bring to boil. Cook for a further 5 minutes and add parsley and season to taste.
5. Bring water to the boil and add the couscous, cover with a lid and allow to settle.
6. Heat oil in a frying pan over high heat and cook lamb for 3 minutes each side.
7. Serve the lamb with ratatouille and couscous.

Lunch for tomorrow: Lamb ratatouille

Save some lamb ratatouille for tomorrow's lunch!

Recipes for Week 2: Day 2

Your food diary:

Meal   Time   Description

Breakfast:

Snacks:

Lunch:

Snacks:

Dinner:

Snacks:

BREAKFAST

Muesli with fresh fruit

240g muesli (60g per person)
Serving of milk (soya/rice/oat or skimmed milk)
Fruit of your choice, cut into chunks (1 piece of fruit per person)

1. Place muesli in a bowl, add milk.
2. Serve with fruit.

LUNCH

Lamb with feta/goat's cheese

4 pitta breads, 1 per person (serve hot or cold)
Ratatouille and sauce from previous meal
Lettuce, generous amount of
Lamb
Feta/goat's cheese, small amount
Soya/plain yoghurt

1. Slice open pitta bread and fill with lamb, ratatouille, salad and sprinkle with feta/goat's cheese.
2. Drizzle the soya/plain yoghurt over the top.

DINNER

Chilli fish

4 plaice fillets
1 tablespoon olive oil
1 tablespoon fresh coriander
2 tablespoons lime juice
300ml water
2 tablespoons tomato puree

1 tablespoon chilli sauce
1cm ginger, grated
1 tablespoon white wine vinegar
1 teaspoon muscovado sugar
Lemon wedges, to serve
Serve with brown rice

1. Place fish in a dish, add olive oil, coriander and lime juice and coat well. Cover in cling film and place in the fridge to marinate.
2. Preheat the grill to medium heat. Place water, tomato puree, chilli sauce, white wine vinegar, ginger and sugar in small sauce pan. Stir and simmer for 5–8 minutes or until thick.
3. Meanwhile, remove the fish from the marinade and cook under the grill for 5–8 minutes or until the flesh flakes easily.
4. Transfer fish to plates and spoon over the sauce.
5. Serve with brown rice and garnish with lemon wedges.

PREPARE

Lunch for tomorrow: Tuna salad with sweet potato

1. Preheat oven 190°C (375°F)
2. Cut the sweet potatoes into small chunks and drizzle a tablespoon of extra virgin olive oil.
3. Place in oven for 30–40 minutes.
4. Once cooked allow to cool and place into the fridge for ready tommorrow's lunch.

Recipes for Week 2: Day 3

Your food diary:

Meal   Time   Description

Breakfast:

Snacks:

Lunch:

Snacks:

Dinner:

Snacks:

BREAKFAST

Scrambled eggs with wild mushrooms

8 wild mushrooms, large
8 eggs
200ml serving of milk (soya/rice/oat or skimmed milk)
1 tablespoon chives, chopped
2 teaspoons olive oil
Ground black pepper

1. Preheat the grill to high heat. Brush mushrooms with olive oil and season with pepper. Grill for about 10 minutes or until tender.
2. Meanwhile, in a bowl, lightly whisk eggs and milk together and lightly season with black pepper.
3. Heat a non-stick frying pan over medium heat and pour in the egg mixture and cook. Keep stirring until the egg is cooked, then stir in chives. Place eggs on the mushrooms and serve.

LUNCH

Tuna salad with sweet potato

4 sweet potatoes, cooked
4 small tins tuna
1 tablespoon balsamic vinegar
1 tablespoon olive oil

Side salad:
100g of rocket leaves
4 tomatoes, roughly chopped
¼ cucumber, roughly chopped
50g mange-tout
1 red pepper, sliced

1. Preheat oven 190°C (375°F). Cut the sweet potatoes into small chunks and drizzle a tablespoon of exra virgin olive oil and place into oven for 30–40 minutes.
2. Place rocket leaves, mange-tout, tomatoes, cucumber and red pepper in a salad bowl and gently mix with balsamic vinegar and olive and serve with the tuna and sweet potatoes.

DINNER

Turkey stir fry with orange

4 turkey breasts, sliced
1 tablespoon of sesame oil
1 tablespoon olive oil
2 large carrots, thinly sliced
175g small florets of broccoli
2 red peppers, sliced
2 teaspoons ginger, crushed
2 teaspoons garlic, crushed

4 spring onions, finely sliced
1 tablespoon corn flour
Serve with brown rice

For the marinade:
2 tablespoons soy sauce
1 large orange, finely grated and juiced
1 tablespoon whole grain mustard

1. Marinade: mix together the soy sauce, mustard, orange rind and juice into a small bowl. Stir in the turkey and set aside to marinade. Boil the rice.
2. Heat the olive and sesame oil in a wok or large frying pan over high heat. Add the carrots and broccoli and cook for 3 minutes.
3. Remove the turkey from mix and add to the wok. Add the garlic, ginger, spring onions and red pepper and stir fry for another 4 minutes.
4. Mix the corn flour and the reserve of the marinade to make a smooth sauce and pour over the turkey.
5. Stir fry for a further 1–2 minutes until the broccoli is tender, serve immediately with brown rice.

PREPARE

Lunch for tomorrow: Vegetable soup (use ingredients as found in Week 2 Day 4)

1. Bring stock to boil in a large saucepan, add the carrot, celery, onion, parsley and tomatoes and simmer gently for 30 minutes.
2. Stir through the basil and rosemary and season with black pepper.

Recipes for Week 2: Day 4

BREAKFAST

Fruit porridge

240g of porridge oats (60g per person)
2-3 apples, chopped
120ml of water or milk (soya/rice/oat or skimmed milk) -
enough to cover the oats and apples

1. Slowly bring to the boil the water and/or milk in a sauce pan.
2. Add the oats and chopped apples.
3. Cook for 10 minutes, stirring continuously until thickened. If the mixture becomes too thick, add more water or milk. Serve immediately.

LUNCH

Vegetable soup

1 litre vegetable stock
2 carrots, sliced
2 celery sticks, chopped
1 onion, chopped

1 tablespoon fresh parsley, chopped
400g tinned tomatoes
1 tablespoon basil, chopped
1 tablespoon rosemary, finely chopped

1. Bring stock to boil in a large saucepan.
2. Add the carrots, celery, onion, parsley and tomatoes and simmer gently for 30 minutes.
3. Stir through basil and rosemary and season with black pepper.

DINNER

Tuna steak and cannellini bean salad

1 tablespoon pine nuts
4 x 100g tuna steaks
½ tablespoon olive oil
1 garlic clove, crushed
400g white cannellini beans, drained and rinsed

1 tablespoon basil, finely sliced
½ tablespoon parsley
2 spring onions, finely sliced
Generous amount of mixed salad leaves

1. Heat a small non stick frying pan over medium heat and add the pine nuts and stir until toasted and golden, then set aside.
2. Heat a large non stick frying pan over high heat and add the olive oil.
3. Place tuna steaks in frying pan and cook for 2–3 minutes each side. The tuna should still be a little pink in middle. Allow to cool slightly.
4. Place the remaining ingredients and pine nuts in bowl and mix.
5. Serve the tuna with bean salad on the side.

PREPARE

Dinner for tomorrow: Tandoori turkey salad

400g turkey breasts, uncooked
For the Marinade:
1 tablespoon tandoori paste
50g soya/plain yoghurt

1. Mix the tandoori paste and yoghurt in a bowl.
2. Add the turkey and coat thoroughly.
3. Cover and leave refrigerated overnight for tomorrow's dinner.

Recipes for Week 2: Day 5

Your food diary:

Meal   Time   Description

Breakfast:

Snacks:

Lunch:

Snacks:

Dinner:

Snacks:

BREAKFAST

Fresh fruit and seeds

8 tablespoons soya/plain yoghurt

Sprinkle of sunflower or pumpkin seeds

2 pieces of fruit of your choice per person

1. Mix together the soya/plain yoghurt, seeds and fruit
2. Divide into 4 portions.

LUNCH

Beef salad pitta

4 wholemeal pitta breads (serve hot or cold)

400g cold roast beef, finely sliced

Green salad, generous amounts of

4 large tomatoes, sliced

1 red pepper, sliced

½ red onion, finely sliced

2 tablespoons chopped basil

For the dressing:

2 tablespoons olive oil

1 tablespoon balsamic vinegar

1 clove garlic, crushed

1 teaspoon dijon mustard

Season with black pepper

1. In a small bowl mix together all the dressing ingredients.
2. Put the remaining ingredients in a large salad bowl and mix well.
3. Slice open the pitta bread and fill with beef and salad.
4. Pour the dressing over the top.

DINNER

Tandoori turkey salad

4 sweet potatoes, peeled and chopped

½ tablespoon olive oil

400g turkey breasts

100g baby spinach

4 plum tomatoes, thinly sliced

½ a cucumber

Coriander, small handful

Garnish with lemon wedges

For the marinade:

1 tablespoon tandoori paste

50g of soya/plain yoghurt

For the dressing:

150g of soya/plain yoghurt

2 tablespoons fresh mint

½ tablespoon olive oil

2 tablespoons lemon juice

1. Mix the tandoori paste and soya/plain yoghurt in a bowl.
2. Add the turkey and coat thoroughly. Cover and chill for 30 minutes – leave overnight if you have time.
3. Meanwhile, Preheat the oven to 190°C (375°F).
4. Place sweet potatoes in an ovenproof dish and drizzle with olive oil. Cook for 20–30 minutes or until soft.
5. Preheat grill and cook turkey over a medium heat for 6 minutes each side or until cooked. Remove from the heat and let turkey rest for 5 minutes then slice the turkey into strips.
6. Place the spinach, tomatoes and cucumber in large salad bowl and put turkey strips over the top.
7. Mix the dressing ingredients together in a small bowl and drizzle the dressing over salad.
8. Garnish with coriander and lemon wedges and serve.

PREPARE

Lunch for tomorrow: Bean salad

1. Boil 4 eggs for 6½ minutes.
2. Place in cold water to cool and refrigerate overnight.

Recipes for Week 2: Day 6

Your food diary:

Meal	Time	Description
Breakfast:		
Snacks:		
Lunch:		
Snacks:		
Dinner:		
Snacks:		

Fruit smoothie

2 large mangos, peeled and chopped
4 bananas, chopped
2 handfuls of raspberries

Blend mangos, bananas and raspberries and serve.

Bean salad

4 eggs
2 avocados, stoned and peeled
400g tinned kidney beans
400g tinned pinto beans
1 red onion, finely sliced
Coriander, large handful chopped
250g cherry tomatoes, halved

For the dressing:
1 red chilli, finely sliced
½ teaspoon ground cumin
1 tablespoon of lime juice
3 tablespoons olive oil

1. Boil eggs for 6 ½ minutes, then place in cold water to cool.
2. Slice avocados and place in bowl with the beans, onions, coriander and tomatoes.
3. Mix the dressing ingredients in a small bowl.
4. Once eggs have cooled but are still warm, peel off shells and cut into quarters.
5. Mix the salad with the dressing and place the eggs on top and serve.

Swordfish with mediterranean vegetables

2 tablespoons olive oil
1 cloves of garlic, chopped
2 teaspoons balsamic vinegar
1 tablespoon parsley, chopped
1 tablespoon basil
Juice of ½ lemon
4 x 200g swordfish steaks
Garnish with lemon wedges

Side vegetables:
1 red pepper, sliced and deseeded
1 yellow pepper, sliced and deseeded
2 courgettes, sliced
1 red onion, sliced
10 new potatoes, thinly sliced

1. Preheat the grill to high.
2. Add new potatoes in a baking tray and drizzle with olive oil. Place under the grill for 10–15 minutes.
3. Add the peppers, courgettes and onion into a bowl with half the olive oil and mix.
4. Transfer vegetables to the grill with the new potatoes and cook for 3–5 minutes turning occasionally until slightly charred.
5. Place cooked vegetables and potatoes into a bowl.
6. To make the mixture for the fish, add garlic, balsamic vinegar, parsley, basil, lemon juice and rest of olive oil and mix together in another bowl.
7. Place fish in foil, add the mixture and wrap.
8. Grill the fish for 2–3 minutes each side or until cooked.
9. Divide vegetables and new potatoes between 4 plates and place fish on top.
10. Garnish with lemon wedges and serve immediately.

Recipes for Week 2: Day 7

Your food diary:

Meal   Time Description

Breakfast:

Snacks:

Lunch:

Snacks:

Dinner:

Snacks:

BREAKFAST

Omelette

8 eggs (2 eggs per person)
4 tablespoons of cold water
8 teaspoons of extra virgin olive oil cold pressed
400g lean ham
1 courgette, finely sliced
4 spring onions, finely chopped

1. Cook one omelette at a time, beat the eggs with some water in a bowl.
2. Heat the extra virgin olive oil in a non stick pan over a high heat and pour in the eggs. Cook for 2 minutes or until the mixture just begins to set.
3. Place ham and courgette on top of the egg mixture and cook until omelette has set.
4. Sprinkle on the spring onions, fold omelette in half and serve.

LUNCH

Tuna and olive salad

175g/6oz french beans, topped and tailed
350g/12oz fresh tuna steaks
115g baby plum tomatoes, halved
8 anchovy fillets (drained on kitchen paper)
25g/1oz stoned black olives, in brine (drained)
Fresh basil leaves, to garnish

For the dressing:
1 tablespoon olive oil
1 garlic clove, crushed
1 tablespoon lemon juice
1 tablespoon basil leaves, shredded

1. Cook the french beans in a small saucepan of boiling water for 5 minutes, or until slightly tender. Drain well and keep warm.
2. Season the tuna steaks with black pepper and place tuna on grill rack and cook for 4–5 minutes on each side, or cooked through.
3. Drain the tuna on kitchen paper, using a knife and fork, flake the tuna into bite size pieces.
4. Mix the tuna, french beans, tomatoes, anchovies and olives into a bowl and keep warm.
5. Mix all the dressing ingredients together. Pour dressing over tuna salad. Garnish with basil and serve.

DINNER

Hot bean soup with butternut squash

1-2 tablespoons olive oil
1 medium onion, chopped and peeled
2 cloves of garlic, peeled and finely chopped
1 butternut squash, peeled and chopped small
2 large carrots, peeled and chopped
2 celery sticks, trimmed and chopped
1 large courgette, sliced

2 red peppers, deseeded and chopped
1.5 litres (2.5 pints) vegetable stock
50g tinned chickpeas
75g red tinned kidney beans
1 teaspoon cayenne pepper
1 teaspoon turmeric powder

1. Heat the olive oil in large pan over medium heat, add onion and garlic and cook for 2–3 minutes.
2. Add cayenne pepper and turmeric and stir for 2 minutes.
3. Add butternut squash, carrots, and celery and cook for a further 4–5 minutes.
4. Next add the courgette and peppers and cook for 2 minutes.
5. Add in the chickpeas, kidney beans, butternut beans and vegetable stock.
6. Cover the pan with lid and simmer gently for 40 minutes to an 1 hour. Serve and enjoy!

PREPARE

Lunch for tomorrow: Chicken wrap

1. Heat ½ tablespoon extra virgin olive oil in a frying pan over a medium heat.
2. Cook the 4 chicken breasts for 8–12 minutes or until cooked. Allow to cool, then refrigerate.

enjoy your food
week 3

Week 3 Overview

DAY	BREAKFAST	LUNCH	DINNER
1	Fruit salad	Chicken wrap	Lemon sole
2	Fruit porridge	Tuna salad with sweet potato	Chicken hot pot
3	Muesli with fresh fruit	Chicken hot pot	Cod and spinach parcels
4	Wheat biscuits/Shredded Wheat or muesli with fruit	Egg salad	Stir fried pork
5	Fresh fruit and seeds	Salmon salad	Chicken yoghurt
6	Omelette	Butternut squash and coriander soup	Limed tuna steaks
7	Fruit smoothie	Chicken salad with pitta bread	Beef and sweet potato pie

Snack list

- **Fruits:**

    Melon, mango or coconut – 1 to share

    Peach, plum, or kiwi – 1

    Pineapple – 1 to share (I had 2 slices a week)

    Orange or nectarine – 1

    Berries (blackberries, goji, blueberries, raspberries or strawberries) – 2 portions

    Pear – 1

    Banana – 5

    Apple – 5

- **Dr Karg crackers** – 3
- **Crackers/flat breads** – 1
- **Small bowl of muesli** (if really hungry) – 2
- **Yoghurt/soya yoghurt** (four dessert spoons) – 1
- **Nuts** (cashew, pine or occasionally mixed nuts) – 2 to 3 handfuls
- **Soya nuts** – after all training sessions 3 to 4 handfuls
- **Seeds** (pumpkin or sunflower) – 2 to 3 handfuls
- **Pitta bread/wrap with salad and protein filling** – 1

I would roughly snack four to five times a day at random intervals. On average however, I snacked at 10.00am, 12.00pm, 2.30pm and 4.00pm. You can use this as a guide, but you do not need to snack five times a day – just when you need to.

Shopping List
Week 3

Carbohydrates:

1 bag of brown rice
240g of Jordans muesli
10 new potatoes
1 bag of pine nuts
8 wholemeal or brown pitta breads
560g porridge oats
1 bag of rice noodles
1 bag of sunflower and pumpkin seeds
4 organic tortilla wraps
6 sweet potatoes
Wheat biscuits/Shredded wheat

Dairy and non-dairy alternatives:

12 eggs
680ml skimmed/Alpro soya/rice /oat milk
1.7kg Alpro soya yoghurt

Fish:

200g x 4 cod fillets
4 lemon sole
175g tuna steaks

Meat:

400g lean minced beef
12 chicken breasts
800g chicken thigh fillets
400g lean ham
450g pork fillets
4 turkey breasts
1.4kg rack of veal

Fruit drinks

1 carton Tropicana/Innocent fruit drink

Fruit:

3 apples
2 apricots
8 bananas
1 lemon
2 limes
3 oranges
2 mangos
1 melon
1 large pineapple
1 punnet of raspberries

Vegetables:

2 avocados
115g baby corn
4 baby gem lettuce
600g baby spinach
400g bamboo shoots
175g broccoli
200g button mushrooms
300g cherry tomatoes
2 butternut squash
8 carrots
7 celery sticks
2 courgettes
1 cucumber
3 leeks
3 lettuces
450g mange tout
11 onions
225g frozen peas
4 plum tomatoes
3 red onions
4 red peppers
14 red tomatoes
100g rocket salad
13 spring onions
4 yellow peppers

Herbs:

Basil
Black pepper
Coriander
Cumin
Dill
Fresh ginger
1 garlic clove
1 lemon thyme sprig
Nutmeg
Parsley
Rosemary
Turmeric

Other:

Balsamic vinegar
Beef stock
Chicken stock
Chinese white wine vinegar
Cold pressed extra virgin olive oil
Corn flour
Plain flour
Dark soy sauce
115ml red wine
Soy sauce
400g tinned tomatoes
Vegetable stock
115ml white wine
White wine vinegar

Snacks:

Fruits
Dr Karg crackers
Crackers/flat breads
Small bowl of muesli
Yoghurt/Alpro soya yoghurt
Nuts (cashew, pine or occasionally mixed nuts)
Soya nuts
Seeds (pumpkin or sunflower)

Recipes for Week 3: Day 1

BREAKFAST

Fruit salad

8 tablespoons soya/plain yoghurt (2 tablespoons per person)

80g oats

60g sunflower seeds or pumpkin seeds

4-5 pieces of fruit (preferably ones in season)

1. Dice fruit into chunks and divide into 4 portions.
2. Add 2 tablespoons of soya/plain yoghurt in each portion and sprinkle with oats and seeds.

LUNCH

Chicken salad wrap

4 chicken breasts, cooked and cut into strips

4 tortilla organic whole wheat wraps (served hot or cold)

200g mixed salad

4-5 tomatoes, sliced

1 red onion, finely chopped

1 yellow pepper, cut into strips

2 tablespoons of soya/plain yoghurt

1. Heat ½ tablespoon extra virgin olive oil in a frying pan over a medium heat.
2. Cook 4 chicken breasts for 8–12 minutes or until cooked.
3. Place mixed salad, red onion, yellow pepper, tomatoes and chicken in salad bowl and mix well.
4. Place tortilla wraps on plates, add mixture from salad bowl and roll wrap.
5. Drizzle over soya/plain yoghurt.

DINNER

Lemon sole

1 small onion, finely chopped

4 lemon sole fillets (175g each)

2 garlic cloves, sliced thinly

4 lemon thyme sprigs

1 lemon, grated rind and juice

2 tablespoons olive oil

Serve with brown rice and vegetables of your choice (courgettes, spring onions, etc)

1. Preheat oven to 180°C (350°F). Boil the rice and grill the vegetables you have chosen.
2. Place sole fillets in large ovenproof dish and sprinkle onion on top. Add garlic and 2 lemon thyme sprigs on top of the fillets and season with pepper.
3. Mix lemon juice and olive oil in a small bowl and pour over fish.
4. Bake in oven for 15 minutes or until fish flakes easily.
5. Sprinkle on the lemon rind and the rest of the lemon thyme sprigs and serve with rice.

PREPARE

Lunch for tomorrow: Tuna salad with sweet potato

1. Preheat oven 190°C (375°F).
2. Dice the sweet potatoes and drizzle a tablespoon of extra virgin olive oil over the top, then place into oven for 30–40 minutes.
3. Once cooked, allow to cool then place into the fridge for tommorrow's lunch.

Recipes for Week 3: Day 2

BREAKFAST

Fruit porridge

240g of porridge oats (60g per person)

2-3 apples, chopped

120ml of water or milk (soya/rice/oat or skimmed milk) –
enough to cover the oats and apples

1. Slowly bring to the boil the water and/or milk in a sauce pan.
2. Add the oats and chopped apples.
3. Cook for 10 minutes, stirring continuously until thickened. If the mixture becomes too thick, add more water or milk.
4. Serve immediately.

LUNCH

Tuna salad with sweet potato

4 sweet potatoes

4 small tins tuna

100g rocket leaves

4 tomatoes, roughly chopped

¼ cucumber, roughly chopped

50g mange-tout

1 red pepper, sliced

1 tablespoon balsamic vinegar

1 tablespoon olive oil

1. Preheat oven 190°C (375°F).
2. Dice the sweet potatoes and drizzle a tablespoon of exra virgin olive oil over the top, then place into oven for 30–40 minutes.
3. Place rocket leaves, mange-tout, tomatoes, cucumber and red pepper in a salad bowl.
4. Add the balsamic vinegar and olive oil to salad and mix well.
5. Serve with the tuna and sweet potatoes.

DINNER

Chicken hot pot

Olive oil, 2 tablespoons

800g chicken thigh fillets, diced

225ml chicken stock

400g tinned chopped tomatoes

115ml white wine,

2 cloves garlic, crushed

Corn flour

2 tablespoons rosemary, chopped

2 carrots, finely sliced

2 celery sticks, chopped

2 leeks, washed and sliced

Serve with Charlotte potatoes

1. Heat olive oil in large pan over high heat.
2. Add the chicken in batches and cook for 5 minutes or until brown and remove from pan once cooked.
3. Reduce heat to medium, add the leeks and cook for 8 minutes or until soft.
4. Add the carrots, celery and garlic and cook for a further 10–12 minutes until soft.
5. Add the stock, wine and tomatoes and bring to boil.
6. Reduce heat to low and return chicken with some corn flour (to thicken the sauce) and simmer gently for 35 minutes.
7. Add herbs to taste and serve with Charlotte potatoes.

PREPARE

Lunch for tomorrow: Hot pot chicken

1. Cook 4 chicken breasts (1 per person) for tomorrow's lunch or use any remaining chicken from today's hot pot.
2. Heat ½ tablespoon extra virgin olive oil in a frying pan over a medium heat.
3. Cook the chicken for 8–12 minutes or until cooked.

Your food diary:

Meal Time Description

Breakfast:

Snacks:

Lunch:

Snacks:

Dinner:

Snacks:

Your food diary:

Meal   Time   Description

Breakfast:

Snacks:

Lunch:

Snacks:

Dinner:

Snacks:

Recipes for Week 3: Day 3

BREAKFAST

Muesli with fresh fruit

240g muesli (60g per person)
Serving of milk (soya/rice/oat or skimmed milk)
Fruit of your choice, cut into chunks (1 piece of fruit per person)

1. Place muesli in a bowl, add milk.
2. Serve with fruit.

LUNCH

Chicken hot pot

4 chicken breasts, cooked and diced
4 wholemeal pitta bread (served hot or cold)
Sauce from last night's dinner
Lettuce, 4 handfuls washed and chopped

1 red pepper, sliced
1 yellow pepper, sliced
½ red onion, finely sliced

1. Use any remaining chicken and sauce from the hot pot.
2. Heat ½ tablespoon extra virgin olive oil in a frying pan over a medium heat.
3. Cook the chicken for 8–12 minutes or until cooked.
4. Slice open the pitta bread and fill with chicken and salad and pour in the sauce.
5. Serve with salad.

DINNER

Cod and spinach parcels

4 x 200g cod (or barramundi), with skin removed
200g baby spinach leaves
1 tablespoon, ginger
3 spring onions, finely sliced

2 tablespoons soy sauce
Coriander, handful
Lime wedges
Serve with broccoli and brown rice

1. Preheat oven to 220°C (425°F). Boil the rice and broccoli.
2. Get a large sheet of foil and place half of the spinach leaves in the middle. Add a piece of fish on top then sprinkle with a quarter of ginger, spring onion and drizzle with 2 teaspoons of soy sauce.
3. Wrap the fish in the foil, folding the corners in to ensure the foil is well sealed.
4. Repeat this process with the rest of the fish for each person.
5. Place the 4 parcels in a baking dish and bake for 15 minutes.
6. Carefully open each parcel and slide contents onto plate.
7. Serve with broccoli and brown rice.

PREPARE

Lunch for tomorrow: Egg salad

1. Boil 4 eggs for 6½ minutes then place in cold water to cool.
2. Allow to cool and refrigerate.

Recipes for Week 3: Day 4

Wheat biscuits, Shredded Wheat or muesli with a fruit

560ml milk (soya/rice/oat or skimmed milk)
2-3 wheat biscuits/Shredded Wheat or 240g of Muesli, (60g per person)
1 piece of fruit of your choice

Place oats or cereal in a bowl add milk and serve with fruit.

Your food diary:

Meal	Time	Description
Breakfast:		
Snacks:		
Lunch:		
Snacks:		
Dinner:		
Snacks:		

Egg salad

4 baby gem lettuce
200g baby spinach
150g cherry tomatoes, halved
4 shelled hard boiled eggs, cut into quarters
½ cucumber, sliced
1 yellow pepper, deseeded and sliced

For the dressing:

1 tablespoon dijon mustard
1 tablespoon olive oil
2 teaspoons cider vinegar
1 teaspoon water

1. Arrange the lettuce, spinach, tomatoes, yellow pepper, and cucumber on plates.
2. Mix the mustard and water add mix in the olive oil and vinegar into a small bowl.
3. Put the eggs on top of the salad, drizzle with the dressing and serve.

Stir fried pork

450g/1ib lean pork fillet, cut into strips
1 tablespoon, olive oil,
16 button mushrooms
115g/4 oz baby corn
1 Garlic clove, finely chopped
Fresh ginger, 2.5cm finely chopped
400g mange-tout
400g/14oz bamboo shoots, drained and sliced
2 teaspoons dark soy sauce
2 teaspoons chinese rice wine
225ml/8 fl oz vegetable or chicken stock

2 teaspoons corn flour
1 tablespoon water
1 carrot, finely sliced
1–2 spring onions, trimmed and cut length ways
Serve with rice or rice noodles

For the marinade:

1 tablespoon dark soy sauce
1 tablespoon chinese rice wine
2 teaspoons corn flour
Pepper

1. Mix the marinade ingredients together in a dish and season with pepper.
2. Add the pork to the marinade, cover and chill for 20 minutes.
3. Blanch the baby corn in boiling water for a few minutes.
4. Drain and refresh in cold water.
5. Heat half the olive oil, in a Preheated wok and add the pork. Stir fry for 5 minutes until browned. Remove and reserve.
6. Wipe the wok and add the remaining oil and heat. Next, place in the garlic and cook until golden, adding the ginger, mange-tout, bamboo shoots and mushrooms and fry for 3 minutes.
7. Stir in the soy sauce, chinese rice wine, stock and the reserved liquid from pork.
8. Cook for 2–3 minutes then mix the corn flour and water and stir until thickened.
9. Return the pork to the heat stirring in the carrot.
10. Garnish with spring onions and serve with rice or rice noodles.

Recipes for Week 3: Day 5

Fresh fruit and seeds

8 tablespoons soya/plain yoghurt

Sprinkle of sunflower or pumpkin seeds

2 pieces of fruit of your choice per person

1. Mix together the soya/plain yoghurt, seeds and fruit
2. Divide into 4 portions.

Salmon salad

200g mixed salad leaves

¼ cucumber, roughly chopped

4 cooked poach salmon fillets, bite size pieces

2 yellow peppers, sliced

2 tablespoons coriander chopped

250g cherry tomatoes, halved

For the dressing:

500g soya/plain yoghurt

2 tablespoons coriander, chopped

1 garlic clove, finely chopped

4 teaspoons lemon juice

1 teaspoon cumin, ground

1. For the dressing, place all ingredients in a bowl and mix together; season with black pepper.
2. Cover and refrigerate for 5–10 minutes before using. (If the sauce is too thick, add some water to thin out).
3. Arrange salad leaves, cherry tomatoes, spring onions, salmon, cucumber and yellow pepper in a salad bowl and toss.
4. Add salmon on top of salad
5. Drizzle the dressing over and serve.

Chicken yoghurt

1 tablespoon plain flour

4 lean chicken breasts, diced skinless

1 tablespoon olive oil

8 onions, small chopped

2 garlic cloves, crushed

225ml/8 fl oz chicken stock

2 carrots, chopped

2 celery sticks, chopped

225g frozen peas

1 yellow pepper, sliced and deseeded

115g button mushrooms, sliced

125ml/4fl oz low fat soya/plain yoghurt

3 tablespoons fresh parsley, chopped

Serve with new potatoes

1. Spread flour over a dish and season with pepper and add chicken. Coat with flour.
2. Heat olive oil in large saucepan and add the onions and garlic and cook over low heat, stirring occasionally for 5 minutes.
3. Add chicken and cook for 10 minutes continuously stirring.
4. Stir in the chicken stock, carrots, peas and celery.
5. Bring to boil and then reduce the heat; cover and simmer for 5 minutes.
6. Add the peppers and mushrooms, cover and simmer for a further 10 minutes.
7. Stir in the soya/plain yoghurt and chopped parsley and cook for a further 1–2 minutes.
8. Serve with new potatoes.

Recipes for Week 3: Day 6

BREAKFAST

Omelette

8 eggs (2 eggs per person)
4 tablespoons of cold water
8 teaspoons of extra virgin olive oil cold pressed
400g lean ham
1 courgette, finely sliced
4 spring onions, finely chopped

1. Cook one omelette at a time, beat the eggs with some water in a bowl.
2. Heat the extra virgin olive oil in a non stick pan over a high heat and pour in the eggs. Cook for 2 minutes or until the mixture just begins to set.
3. Place ham and courgette on top of the egg mixture and cook until omelette has set.
4. Sprinkle on the spring onions, fold omelette in half and serve.

LUNCH

Butternut squash and coriander soup

900ml chicken stock
1kg butternut squash, peeled and chopped
1 onion, roughly chopped
2 carrots, roughly chopped
2 celery sticks, roughly chopped

1 garlic clove, finely chopped
1 teaspoon paprika
½ teaspoon turmeric
½ teaspoon ground coriander
½ teaspoon ground nutmeg

1. In a large saucepan, bring chicken stock to boil. Add vegetables and spices and bring back to boil. Reduce heat and simmer for 20 minutes, or until vegetables are soft.
2. Allow to cool, and then blend. Reheat soup and serve.

DINNER

Limed tuna steaks

4 x 175g tuna steaks, trim the skin
2 teaspoons, olive oil
½ teaspoon Lime, grated rind
1 garlic glove, crushed
1 teaspoon ground cumin
1 teaspoon ground coriander
1 tablespoon lime juice
Small handful of fresh coriander, chopped
Serve with Salad

For the relish:
2 avocados, peeled and chopped
1 tablespoon lime juice
½ red onion, cut finely
2 tomatoes, chopped

1. Mix together the avocados, lime juice, red onion and tomatoes in a small bowl.
2. To make the paste, mix lime rind, olive oil, garlic, ground cumin, ground coriander in bowl.
3. Spread paste thinly on both sides of the tuna while heating a non-stick pan until hot and press the tuna steaks into pan to seal them.
4. Reduce heat and cook for 5 minutes. Turn tuna steaks over and cook for a further 4–5mins, or until cooked through.
5. Remove tuna from pan and drain on kitchen paper.
6. Transfer fish to plates, serve with salad and relish.
7. Sprinkle 1 tablespoon of lime juice over the top, garnish with fresh coriander and serve immediately.

Your food diary:

Meal   Time   Description

Breakfast:

Snacks:

Lunch:

Snacks:

Dinner:

Snacks:

Recipes for Week 3: Day 7

BREAKFAST

Fruit smoothie

2 large mangos, peeled and chopped

4 bananas, chopped

2 handfuls of raspberries

Blend mangos, bananas and raspberries and serve.

LUNCH

Chicken salad with pitta

4 pitta breads, hot or cold

½ tablespoon olive oil

4 lean chicken breasts, slice into strips

4 tablespoons fresh basil, chopped

1 red pepper

2 spring onions, finely chopped

150g cherry tomatoes, halved

2 tablespoons pine nuts

200g baby spinach

For the dressing:

¼ of a cucumber, finely grated

4 tablespoons soya/plain yogurt

1 tablespoons olive oil

1 teaspoon balsamic vinegar

2 teaspoons black pepper

2 teaspoons dried dill

1. Pour the olive oil in a frying pan or wok, on a medium heat.
2. Add chicken strips and cook for 8 minutes, or until golden brown. Keep stirring.
3. Add the red pepper, spring onions, tomatoes and pine nuts and cook for a few minutes, while stirring.
4. Place all dressing ingredients in a small bowl and mix well.
5. Slice open the pitta bread and add the chicken, vegetables and spinach. Drizzle over dressing and garnish with basil.

DINNER

Beef and sweet potato pie

800g lean minced beef

2 tablespoons olive oil

1 onion, finely chopped

1 leek, finely chopped

1 carrot, finely chopped

1 stick celery, finely chopped

4 tomatoes, diced

2 sweet potatoes, peeled and chopped

1 medium butternut squash, peeled and chopped

2 cloves of garlic, finely chopped

115ml beef stock

1 tablespoon flour

115ml red wine

1 tablespoon rosemary, chopped

1. Preheat the oven to 180°C (350°F). Heat a large pan of water, boil the sweet potatoes and butternut squash for 10 minutes, or until soft when pierced with knife.
2. Heat a large pan, add olive oil and brown the mince in small batches.
3. Once the mince is cooked, add the onion, leek, carrot, celery, garlic and cook for 4 minutes.
4. Add stock, flour, wine, tomatoes and rosemary and bring to boil. Simmer for 25 minutes.
5. Mash the Sweet Potatoes and butternut squash in a bowl.
6. Put mince mixture in large ovenproof dish and place mash on top.
7. Cook for 20 minutes and serve with salad.

PREPARE

Lunch for tomorrow: Bean salad

1. Boil 4 eggs for 6½ minutes. Place in cold water to cool then refrigerate.

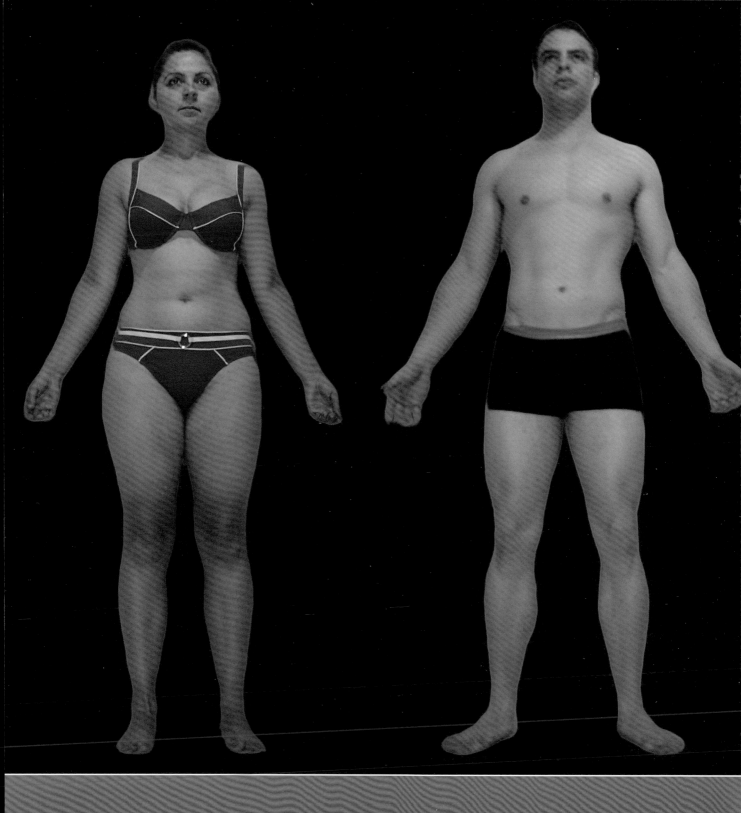

enjoy your food
week 4

Week 4 Overview

DAY	BREAKFAST	LUNCH	DINNER
1	Fresh fruit and seeds	Bean salad	Mediterranean steaks
2	Wheat biscuits/Shredded Wheat or muesli with a piece of fruit	Tuna salad	Stir fried turkey ginger
3	Fruit salad	Beetroot soup	Baked trout
4	Fruit porridge	Chicken wrap	Pork and baked apples
5	Muesli and fresh fruit	Mackerel and potato salad	Tuna pak choi
6	Omelette	Tomato and pepper soup.	Ratatouille lamb chops
7	Fruit smoothie	Tuna and olive salad	Lemon roasted chicken

Snack list

- **Fruits:**

  Melon, mango or coconut – 1 to share

  Peach, plum, or kiwi – 1

  Pineapple – 1 to share (I had 2 slices a week)

  Orange or nectarine – 1

  Berries (blackberries, goji, blueberries, raspberries or strawberries) – 2 portions

  Pear – 1

  Banana – 5

  Apple – 5

- **Dr Karg crackers** – 3
- **Crackers/flat breads** – 1
- **Small bowl of muesli** (if really hungry) – 2
- **Yoghurt/soya yoghurt** (four dessert spoons) – 1
- **Nuts** (cashew, pine or occasionally mixed nuts) – 2 to 3 handfuls
- **Soya nuts** – after all training sessions 3 to 4 handfuls
- **Seeds** (pumpkin or sunflower) – 2 to 3 handfuls
- **Pitta bread/wrap with salad and protein filling** – 1

I would roughly snack four to five times a day at random intervals. On average however, I snacked at 10.00am, 12.00pm, 2.30pm and 4.00pm. You can use this as a guide, but you do not need to snack five times a day – just when you need to.

Shopping List
Week 4

Carbohydrates:

400g baked potatoes
1 bag of brown rice
810g kidney beans
240g of Jordans muesli
400g pinto beans
400g new potatoes
520g porridge oats
1 bag of rice noodles
1 bag of sunflower and pumpkin
 seeds
4 organic tortilla wraps
1 bag of sesame seeds
8 sweet potatoes
Wheat biscuits/Shredded wheat

Dairy and non-dairy alternatives:

12 eggs
680ml skimmed/Alpro soya/rice
 /oat milk
1.7kg Alpro soya yoghurt

Fish:

8 anchovy fillets
4 x 200g cod fillets
4 cooked mackerel
1150g tuna steaks
4 tins tuna
4 whole trout

Meat:

4 chicken breasts
1 large whole chicken
800g pork fillet
400g lean ham
800g lamb chop
800g pork fillet
4 turkey breasts

Fruit:

12 apples
8 bananas
1 punnet of blueberries
5 lemon
2 limes
2 mangos
1 melon
1 punnet of raspberries
1 punnet of strawberries

Vegetables:

4 aubergines
2 avocados
8 asparagus
500g raw beetroot
16 x 25g black olives
500g cherry tomatoes
2 carrots
2 celery sticks
4 courgettes
½ cucumber
50g french beans
175g green beans
2 lettuces
50g mange tout
7 onions
3 pak choi
4 parsnips
50g frozen peas
115g plum tomatoes
3 red onions
7 red peppers
11 + 750g red tomatoes
100g rocket salad
200g savoy cabbage
1 turnip
1 yellow pepper

Herbs:

Basil
1 Bay leaf
Black pepper
Black peppercorns
2 cardamom pods
Chilli powder
Chives
Cinnamon
Coriander
Coriander seeds
Cumin
Fresh ginger
Garam masala
1 garlic clove
Ground fennel
Mint
Oregano
Parsley
Red chilli
Rosemary

Other:

Balsamic vinegar
Chicken stock
Chinese white wine vinegar
Cold pressed extra virgin olive oil
Corn flour
Dijon mustard
Fish stock
Peanut oil
Red wine vinegar
Sun dried tomatoes
Soy sauce
400g tinned tomatoes
Tomato puree
Vegetable stock
White wine vinegar

Snacks:

Fruit
Dr Karg crackers
Crackers/flat breads
Small bowl of muesli
Yoghurt/Alpro soya yoghurt
Nuts (cashew, pine or
 occasionally mixed nuts)
Soya nuts
Seeds (pumpkin or sunflower)

Fruit drinks

1 carton Tropicana/Innocent fruit
drink

Recipes for Week 4: Day 1

Your food diary:

Meal   Time   Description

Breakfast:

Snacks:

Lunch:

Snacks:

Dinner:

Snacks:

BREAKFAST

Fresh fruit and seeds

8 tablespoons of soya/plain yoghurt

Sprinkle of sunflower or pumpkin seeds

2 pieces of fruit of your choice per person

1. Mix together the soya/plain yoghurt, seeds and fruit.
2. Divide into 4 portions.

LUNCH

Bean salad

4 eggs

2 avocados, stoned and peeled

400g tinned kidney beans

400g tinned pinto beans

1 red onion, finely sliced

Chopped coriander, large handful

250g cherry tomatoes, halved

For the dressing:

1 red chilli, finely sliced

½ teaspoon ground cumin

1 tablespoon lime juice

3 tablespoons olive oil

1. Boil eggs for 6½ minutes, then place in cold water to cool.
2. Slice avocados and place in bowl with the beans, onions, coriander and tomatoes.
3. Mix the dressing ingredients in a small bowl.
4. Once eggs have cooled but are still warm, peel off shells and cut into quarters.
5. Mix the salad with the dressing and place the eggs on top and serve.

DINNER

Mediterranean steaks

4 cod steaks – 140g per steak

150ml fish stock

1 bay leaf

6 black peppercorns

Lemon rind

Lemon wedges

1 small onion, sliced

Parsley

For the sauce:

400g chopped tomatoes canned

1 garlic clove, finely chopped

1 tablespoon sun dried tomato paste

16 black olives (optional)

Serve with couscous

1. To make the sauce, place the chopped tomatoes, garlic, tomato paste, olives in a large heavy base saucepan over a low heat. Heat gently, stirring occasionally.
2. Meanwhile, place the fish in a shallow ovenproof casserole dish and pour over the fish stock and add the peppercorns, bay leaf, lemon rind and onion. Bring to boil, cover and simmer for 10 minutes.
3. Transfer cod to a serving plate and keep warm while water boils for the couscous.
4. Next, sieve the fish stock into the sauce and stir over a medium heat until reduced.
5. Pour the sauce over the fish, garnish with parsley and lemon wedges.

PREPARE

Lunch for tomorrow: Tuna salad

1. Preheat oven 190°C (375°F).
2. Cut the sweet potatoes into small chunks and drizzle a tablespoon of exra virgin olive oil over the top, then place into oven for 30–40 minutes.
3. Once cooked place and cooled place into the fridge for tommorrow's lunch.

Recipes for Week 4: Day 2

BREAKFAST

Wheat biscuits, Shredded Wheat or muesli with a fruit

560ml milk (soya/rice/oat milk)
2-3 wheat biscuits/Shredded Wheat or 240g of Muesli, (60g per person)
1 piece of fruit of your choice

Place oats or cereal in a bowl add and serve with fruit.

LUNCH

Tuna salad

4 cooked sweet potatoes
4 small tinned tuna
1 tablespoon balsamic vinegar
1 tablespoon olive oil

Side salad:
100g of rocket leaves
4 tomatoes, roughly chopped
¼ cucumber, roughly chopped
50g mange-tout
1 red pepper, sliced

1. Preheat oven 190°C (375°F).
2. Cut the sweet potatoes into small chunks, drizzle olive oil over the top and place into the oven for 30–40 minutes.
3. Once cooked, allow to cool and place into the fridge for tommorows lunch.
4. Place rocket leaves, mange-tout, tomatoes, cucumber and red pepper in a salad bowl and gently mix with balsamic vinegar and olive. Serve with the tuna and sweet potatoes.

DINNER

Stir fried turkey ginger

2 teaspoons sesame seeds
1 tablespoon sesame oil
800g skinless turkey breasts, cut into thin strips
1 onion, quartered
1 red pepper, deseeded and sliced
2 tablespoons soy sauce

Chinese rice wine, Splash of
1 pak choi, halved
1 x 3cm ginger
1 x garlic clove, crushed
1 red chilli, finely sliced
Serve with brown rice

1. Heat a wok/large frying pan over medium heat, add the sesame seeds, stir until lightly toasted and then set aside.
2. Steam pak choi in a steamer for 2–3 minutes, then remove and set aside. Boil water for the rice.
3. Add the turkey to the wok/frying pan and stir fry for 6–8 minutes, or until the turkey is cooked. Remove from wok and set aside. Wipe out wok with paper towel.
4. Return wok to heat and add the rest of the sesame oil with the ginger, garlic, chilli, onion and red pepper and stir fry for 2 minutes.
5. Return turkey to wok, add rice wine, soy sauce and stir. Add pak choi and stir.
6. Serve with rice and a sprinkle the toasted sesame seeds.

PREPARE

Lunch for tomorrow: Beetroot soup

1. Put onions, carrot, turnips, celery, beetroot, garlic and vegetable stock in large pan.
2. Bring to boil and simmer for 30 minutes.
3. Add the potatoes, cabbage, beans and simmer for a further 20–30 minutes or until potatoes are tender.
4. Stir in the vinegar and allow to cool, then refrigerate overnight and serve for tomorrow's lunch.

Recipes for Week 4: Day 3

Your food diary:

Meal   Time   Description

Breakfast:

Snacks:

Lunch:

Snacks:

Dinner:

Snacks:

BREAKFAST

Fruit salad

8 tablespoons soya/plain yoghurt (2 tablespoons per person)

80g oats

60g sunflower seeds or pumpkin seeds

4–5 pieces of fruit (preferably ones in season)

1. Dice fruit into chunks and divide into 4 portions.
2. Add 2 tablespoons of yoghurt in each portion and sprinkle with oats and seeds.

LUNCH

Beetroot soup

2 onions, peeled and roughly chopped

2 large carrot, peeled and roughly chopped

1 large turnip peeled and roughly chopped

2 celery sticks, roughly chopped

500g raw beetroot, peeled and chopped

400g potatoes, washed and chopped

200g savoy cabbage

3 garlic cloves, finely sliced

2 litres of vegetable stock

410g tin kidney beans

1 tablespoon red wine vinegar

150g soya/plain yoghurt

1. Put onions, carrots, turnips, celery, beetroot, garlic and vegetable stock in large pan.
2. Bring to boil and simmer for 30 minutes.
3. Add the potatoes, cabbage, beans and simmer for a further 20–30 minutes or until potatoes are tender.
4. Stir in the vinegar and serve soup in bowls and stir in the yoghurt.

DINNER

Baked trout

4 sweet potatoes, roughly chopped

1 courgette, roughly chopped

2 red peppers, roughly chopped

250g cherry tomatoes

1 medium red onion, roughly chopped

4 fresh trout, gutted

Black pepper

2 teaspoons coriander

1 teaspoon cinnamon

2 teaspoons oregano

2 teaspoons basil

1 clove garlic, finely chopped

1 tablespoon olive oil

1. Preheat the oven to 190°C (375°F).
2. Pre-boil the sweet potatoes in saucepan of water, heat until potatoes are slightly soft and drain water.
3. Place the sweet potatoes, courgette, tomatoes red pepper, all the herbs, garlic and onion in a baking dish and drizzle over the olive oil.
4. Bake for 10–15 minutes, or until the vegetables are cooked, stirring vegetables occasionally.
5. Meanwhile, Preheat grill to medium/high and place the fish on grill tray.
6. Drizzle over a little olive oil and season with black pepper and cook for 5–6 minutes each side, or until fish is cooked.
7. Arrange vegetables on serving plate and place fish on top.

PREPARE

Lunch for tomorrow: Chicken wrap

1. Heat ½ tablespoon extra virgin olive oil in a frying pan over a medium heat.
2. Cook the chicken for 8–12 minutes, or until cooked.

Recipes for Week 4: Day 4

Your food diary:

Meal   Time   Description

Breakfast:

Snacks:

Lunch:

Snacks:

Dinner:

Snacks:

Fruit porridge

240g of porridge oats (60g per person)
2-3 apples, chopped
120ml of water or milk (soya/rice/oat or skimmed milk) –
   enough to cover the oats and apples

1. Slowly bring to the boil the water and/or milk in a sauce pan.
2. Add the oats and chopped apples.
3. Cook for 10 minutes, stirring continuously until thickened. If the mixture becomes too thick,add more water or milk. Serve immediately.

Chicken wrap

4 cooked chicken breasts, cut into strips
4 tortilla organic whole wheat wraps (served hot or cold)
200g mixed salad
4-5 tomatoes, sliced

1 red onion, finely chopped
1 yellow pepper, sliced
2 tablespoons of soya/plain yoghurt

1. Heat ½ tablespoon extra virgin olive oil in a frying pan over a medium heat.
2. Cook 4 chicken breasts for 8–12 minutes or until cooked.
3. Place mixed salad, red onion, yellow pepper, tomatoes and chicken in salad bowl and mix well.
4. Place tortilla wraps on plates, add mixture from salad bowl and roll wrap.
5. Drizzle over soya/plain yoghurt.

Pork and baked apples

1 x 800g lean pork fillet, remove fat
2 tablespoon ground fennel
2 tablespoons olive oil
2 apples, cored and quartered
2 teaspoons brown sugar

2 tablespoons water
4 parsnips, peeled and chopped into chunks
Rosemary, 4 sprigs
200g green beans

1. Preheat oven to 180°C (350°F).
2. Season the pork with pepper, and roll in the fennel.
3. Wrap in cling film and refrigerate for 10–15 minutes.
4. Heat a large frying pan over a high heat and cook the pork with half the olive oil on each side for 3 minutes, or until golden. Set a side and cover.
5. Place apples in an ovenproof dish, sprinkle the brown sugar and water. Cover with foil and set aside.
6. Place parsnip, rosemary and remaining oil in a baking dish and toss to coat and bake for 10 minutes.
7. Place apples into the oven and at the same time, add the pork to the parsnip dish. After a further 10 minutes cooking, the parsnips should be golden, the pork cooked and the apples soft.
8. Meanwhile, bring a small saucepan of water to boil and add the beans. Cook for 5 minutes.
9. Serve immediately.

Lunch for tomorrow: Mackerel and potato salad

1. Boil or steam new potatoes for 20 minutes or until tender.
2. Allow to cool and then refrigerate.

Your food diary:

Meal   Time   Description

Breakfast:
_____

Snaoko:
_____

Lunch:
_____

Snacks:
_____

Dinner:
_____

Snacks:
_____

Recipes for Week 4: Day 5

BREAKFAST

Muesli and fresh fruit

240g muesli (60g per person)
Serving of milk (soya/rice/oat or skimmed milk)
Fruit of your choice, cut into chunks (1 piece of fruit per person)

1. Place muesli in a bowl, add milk.
2. Serve with fruit.

LUNCH

Mackerel and potato salad

4 mackerel fillets (250g each)
4 teaspoons dijon mustard
Serve with green beans

For the potato salad:
400g new potatoes
4 spring onions, roughly chopped
1 tablespoon fresh dill, chopped
1 tablespoon chives, chopped
1 tablespoon parsley, chopped

1. Steam the potatoes for 20 minutes or until tender.
2. Mix the spring onions, dill, chives, parsley, lemon juice, potatoes and fromage frais in a salad bowl.
3. Preheat the grill to high and wash the mackerel. Pat dry with kitchen towel, making sure the black skin from the gut has been removed.
4. Lay the fillets skin side down and spread the mustard on the flesh.
5. Grill the mackerel for 5 minutes until the flesh is no longer translucent.
6. Serve with potato salad and green beans.

DINNER

Tuna pak choi

4 x 200g tuna steaks
2 teaspoons peanut oil
2 pok choi, leaves separated and washed
4 spring onions, finely sliced
1 tablespoon fresh coriander
1 tablespoon mint leaves
Lime wedges

For the dressing:
2 tablespoon light soy sauce
2 teaspoons lime juice
1 teaspoon ginger, grated

1. In a small bowl mix all the dressing ingredients.
2. Heat frying pan over medium heat and brush tuna steaks with peanut oil.
3. Add tuna to pan and cook 4 minutes each side.
4. Use a steamer to cook pak choi for 2–3 minutes.
5. Arrange the pak choi on a serving plate and place tuna on top.
6. Sprinkle spring onion, coriander, mint and drizzle the dressing on top.
7. Use lime wedges to garnish and serve.

NOTES

Recipes for Week 4: Day 6

BREAKFAST

Omelette

8 eggs (2 eggs per person)
4 tablespoons of cold water
8 teaspoons of extra virgin olive oil cold pressed
400g lean ham
1 courgette, finely sliced
4 spring onions, finely chopped

1. Cook one omelette at a time, beat the eggs with some water in a bowl.
2. Heat the extra virgin olive oil in a non stick pan over a high heat and pour in the eggs. Cook for 2 minutes or until the mixture just begins to set.
3. Place ham and courgette on top of the egg mixture and cook until omelette has set.
4. Sprinkle on the spring onions, fold omelette in half and serve.

LUNCH

Tomato and pepper soup

2 red peppers, deseeded and halved
2 tablespoons olive oil
1 large onion, finely sliced
2 cloves of garlic, crushed

1 tablespoon tomato paste
750g tomatoes, roughly chopped
450ml vegetable stock
Basil, handful

1. Preheat oven 180°C (350°F).
2. Place red peppers in baking tray, skin side up and drizzle with half the olive oil.
3. Roast for 25 minutes, or until soft and remove from oven. Allow to cool slightly, then roughly chop.
4. Heat the rest of the oil in a large saucepan, over medium heat.
5. Add the onion and cook until soft.
6. Add garlic and tomato paste and cook for 2 minutes, stirring continuously.
7. Add red pepper, tomato and stock, cover and simmer for 15 minutes.
8. Allow the soup to cool slightly, and gently stir. Season with basil and serve.

DINNER

Ratatouille lamb chops

8 lean lamb chops, diced
1 tablespoon olive oil
250g couscous
Spices:
1 tablespoon ground pepper
2 teaspoons coriander seeds
1 teaspoon garam masala
1 teaspoon chilli powder

For the ratatouille:
2 teaspoons olive oil
4 baby aubergines
1 onion, finely chopped
1 red pepper, deseeded and sliced
1 courgette, sliced
115ml chicken stock
2 tomatoes, sliced
1 tablespoon parsley, chopped
1 clove garlic, finely chopped

1. Mix all the spices in a bowl and brush the chops with a little olive oil. Coat chops with spice mixture, cover with cling film and refrigerate for 1 hour.
2. To make ratatouille, heat the olive oil in a large frying pan over medium heat. Add aubergines and cook for 4 minutes or until golden.
3. Add onion and garlic and cook until lightly coloured. Next add the red pepper and courgette and cook for further minute.
4. Add chicken stock and tomatoes and bring to boil, cook for a further 5 minutes and add parsley and season to taste.
5. Bring water to a boil and add the couscous, cover with a lid and allow to settle.
6. Heat oil in a frying pan over high heat and cook lamb for 3 minutes each side.
7. Serve the lamb chops with ratatouille and couscous.

Recipes for Week 4: Day 7

Your food diary:

Meal   Time   Description

Breakfast:

Snacks:

Lunch:

Snacks:

Dinner:

Snacks:

Fruit smoothie

2 large mangos, peeled and chopped
4 bananas, chopped
2 handfuls of raspberries

Blend mangos, bananas and raspberries and serve.

Tuna and olive salad

175g french beans, topped and tailed
350g fresh tuna steaks
115g baby plum tomatoes, halved
8 anchovy fillets, drained on kitchen paper
25g stoned black olives in brine, drained
Fresh basil leaves, to garnish

For the dressing:
1 tablespoon olive oil
1 garlic clove, crushed
1 tablespoon lemon juice
1 tablespoon basil leaves, shredded

1. Cook the french beans in a small saucepan of boiling water for 5 minutes, or until slightly tender, drain well and keep warm.
2. Season the tuna steaks with black pepper and place tuna on grill rack and cook for 4–5 minutes on each side, or until cooked through.
3. Drain the tuna on kitchen paper and using a knife and fork, flake the tuna into bite size pieces.
4. Mix the tuna, french beans, tomatoes, anchovies and olives into a bowl and keep warm.
5. Mix all the dressing ingredients together. Pour dressing over tuna salad. Garnish with basil and serve.

Lemon roasted chicken

4 lemons, 2 x grated rinds, 2 x cut into quarters
1 large chicken
1 onion, roughly chopped
50g peas (fresh or frozen)
50g french beans, trimmed

1 courgette, sliced
6-8 asparagus heads, trimmed
600ml chicken stock
Fresh basil, 1 handful chopped
Serve with brown rice

1. Preheat oven to 180°C (350°F). Rub the lemon rind on the chicken and place in a casserole dish
2. Squeeze lemon juice all over the chicken. Add the vegetables and basil around the chicken.
3. Pour over the stock and put the chicken in oven and cook for 1½ hours.
4. Serve with brown rice.

Lunch for tomorrow: Yellow split pea soup

1. Drain water from the split peas.
2. Boil the vegetable stock in a large saucepan and add the split peas, simmer for 25 minutes, removing any scum that may occur from the top.
3. Add the vegetables and simmer for a further 15–20 minutes, or until the vegetables are tender.
4. Remove from heat and allow to cool.
5. Blend soup with food processor or blender.
6. Refrigerate for tomorrow's lunch.

enjoy your food
week 5

Week 5 Overview

DAY	BREAKFAST	LUNCH	DINNER
1	Fresh fruit and seeds	Yellow split pea soup	Prawn stir fry
2	Wheat biscuits/Shredded Wheat or muesli with a piece of fruit	Tuna salad	Lamb stew
3	Muesli and fresh fruit	Lamb pitta	Chicken with lemongrass
4	Fruit porridge	Salmon salad	Fillet of beef
5	Fresh fruit and seeds	Chicken wrap	Barramundi curry
6	Omelette	Beef and beetroot salad	Paella
7	Fruit smoothie	Vegetable soup	Roasted chicken

Snack list

- **Fruits:**

  Melon, mango or coconut – 1 to share

  Peach, plum, or kiwi – 1

  Pineapple – 1 to share (I had 2 slices a week)

  Orange or nectarine – 1

  Berries (blackberries, goji, blueberries, raspberries or strawberries) – 2 portions

  Pear – 1

  Banana – 5

  Apple – 5
- **Dr Karg crackers** – 3
- **Crackers/flat breads** – 1
- **Small bowl of muesli** (if really hungry) – 2
- **Yoghurt/soya yoghurt** (four dessert spoons) – 1
- **Nuts** (cashew, pine or occasionally mixed nuts) – 2 to 3 handfuls
- **Soya nuts** – after all training sessions 3 to 4 handfuls
- **Seeds** (pumpkin or sunflower) – 2 to 3 handfuls
- **Pitta bread/wrap with salad and protein filling** – 1

I would roughly snack four to five times a day at random intervals. On average however, I snacked at 10.00am, 12.00pm, 2.30pm and 4.00pm. You can use this as a guide, but you do not need to snack five times a day – just when you need to.

Shopping List

Week 5

Carbohydrates:

6 baked potatoes
1 bag of brown rice
260g of Jordans muesli
12 new potatoes
480g porridge oats
1 bag of rice noodles
1 bag of sunflower and pumpkin
seeds
4 organic tortilla wraps
5 sweet potatoes
Wheat biscuits/Shredded wheat

Dairy and non-dairy alternatives:

8 eggs
150g greek yoghurt
50g parmesan cheese/goat's
  cheese
1760ml skimmed/Alpro soya/rice
  /oat milk
2.5kg Alpro soya yoghurt

Fish:

800g barramundi fillets
150g calamari
200g mussels
600g raw prawns
4 poached salmon fillets
4 tins tuna
400g white fish of your choice

Meat:

800g beef fillet
400g cooked roast beef
800g chicken on the bone
4 chicken breasts
1 large whole chicken
400g lean ham
800g boneless lamb

Fruit:

7 apples
2 apricots
9 bananas
1 punnet of blueberries
1 bag of green grapes
3 lemons
1 lime
2 peaches
1 punnet of raspberries

Vegetables:

16 asparagus
4 cooked beetroot
125g frozen broad beans
250g broccoli
250g cherry tomatoes
7 carrots
4 celery sticks
1 courgette
½ cucumber
3 lettuce
250g mange tout
175g mushrooms
4 onions
4 parsnips
50g frozen peas
175g runner beans
1 red onion
2 red peppers
16 red tomatoes
150g rocket salad
150g baby spinach
9 spring onions
150g sugar snap peas
1 turnip
1 yellow pepper

Fruit drinks

1 carton Tropicana/Innocent fruit
drink

Herbs:

Basil
3 bay leaves
Black pepper
Coriander
Cumin
6 dill sprigs
1 fennel bulb
Fresh ginger
11 lemongrass stalks
1 garlic clove
Oregano
Paprika
Parsley
6 peppercorns
Red chilli
Rosemary
Saffron
Thyme

Other:

Balsamic vinegar
Chicken stock
Chinese white wine vinegar
Cold pressed extra virgin olive oil
Corn flour
Fish sauce
Prawn paste
Soy sauce
Sugar
800g tinned tomatoes
Tomato puree
Vegetable stock
Worcestershire sauce

Snacks:

Fruits
Dr Karg crackers
Crackers/flat breads
Small bowl of muesli
Yoghurt/Alpro soya yoghurt
Nuts (cashew, pine or
  occasionally mixed nuts)
Soya nuts
Seeds (pumpkin or sunflower)

Recipes for Week 5: Day 1

Your food diary:

Meal   Time   Description

Breakfast:

Snacks:

Lunch:

Snacks:

Dinner:

Snacks:

BREAKFAST

Fresh fruit and seeds

8 tablespoons of soya/plain yoghurt

Sprinkle of sunflower or pumpkin seeds

2 pieces of fruit of your choice per person

1. Mix together the soya/plain yoghurt, seeds and fruit
2. Divide into 4 portions.

LUNCH

Yellow split pea soup

225g yellow split peas
(Pre-soak for 12 hours overnight in cold water)

1.5 litres of vegetable stock

1 onion, peeled and sliced

1 sweet potato, peeled and chopped

3 carrots, trimmed, peeled and sliced

Fresh mint, handful

Baby spinach leaves, 4 handfuls

1. Drain the water from the split peas.
2. Boil the vegetable stock in a large saucepan, add split peas, then simmer for 25 minutes, removing any scum that may occur.
3. Add all the other vegetables and simmer for a further 15–20 minutes, or until vegetables are tender.
4. Remove from heat and allow to cool.
5. Blend soup with food processor or blender.
6. Serve with fresh mint.

DINNER

Prawn stir fry

8 spring onions, finely chopped

1 green pepper, finely chopped

1 red pepper, finely chopped

2 tablespoons olive oil

2 garlic cloves, finely chopped

1 tablespoon ginger, finely cut

200g mange-tout

450g raw prawns, thawed and peeled

4 tablespoons Chinese rice wine

Serve with rice noodles

1. Heat the olive oil in a big frying pan or wok over a medium to high heat.
2. Add the spring onions, garlic, ginger and peppers to pan stir fry for 4 minutes, stirring continuously.
3. Add the mange-tout and prawns and stir fry for 4 minutes or until prawns have change colour.
4. Stir in rice wine.
5. Serve with rice noodles.

PREPARE

Lunch for tomorrow: Tuna salad

1. Preheat oven 190°C (375°F).
2. Cut the sweet potatoes into small chunks and drizzle a tablespoon of exra virgin olive oil over them.
3. Place in oven for 30–40 minutes.
4. Once cooked , allow to cool and refridgerate for tommorow's lunch.

Recipes for Week 5: Day 2

BREAKFAST

Wheat biscuits, Shredded Wheat or muesli with a fruit

560ml milk (soya/rice/oat or skimmed milk)
2-3 wheat biscuits/Shredded Wheat or 240g of Muesli, (60g per person)
1 piece of fruit of your choice

Place oats or cereal in a bowl add milk and serve with fruit.

LUNCH

Tuna salad

4 cooked sweet potatoes
4 small tinned tuna
1 tablespoon balsamic vinegar
1 tablespoon olive oil

Side salad:
100g of rocket leaves
4 tomatoes, roughly chopped
¼ cucumber, roughly chopped
50g mange-tout
1 red pepper, sliced

1. Preheat oven 190°C (375°F).
2. Cut the sweet potatoes into small chunks and drizzle a tablespoon of exra virgin olive oil and place into oven for 30–40 minutes.
3. Once cooked, allow to cool and place into the fridge for tommorrow's lunch.
4. Place rocket leaves, mange-tout, tomatoes, cucumber and red pepper in a salad bowl and gently mix with balsamic vinegar and olive.
5. Serve with the tuna and sweet potatoes.

DINNER

Lamb stew

600g lean boneless lamb, dice into 2.5cm cubes
1 onion, chopped
6 peppercorns
1 fennel bulb
115g mushrooms
1 teaspoon corn flour

1 tablespoon soya milk
150ml soya/plain yoghurt
6 baking potatoes
6 fresh dill sprigs
1 bay leaf
Half a lemon, grated rind and juice

1. Place lamb in large saucepan and cover with cold water.
2. Bring to boil over medium heat, remove any scum that rises to the surface.
3. Add the onion, 2 dill sprigs, bay leaf and peppercorns. Reduce heat, cover and simmer for 45 minutes.
4. Add the fennel, potatoes and mushrooms and simmer for a further 30 minutes, or until lamb is tender.
5. Using a slotted spoon, transfer the lamb, onion, fennel and mushrooms to a dish and keep warm.
6. Sieve the cooking liquid and reserve 300ml. Pour the reserved cooking liquid into a pan and bring to boil. Mix the corn flour and milk until smooth, then add to the cooking liquid.
7. Reduce the heat and simmer for 5 minutes, keep stirring until thickened.
8. Add the lemon rind and juice to the sauce.
9. Return the lamb, onion, fennel, and mushrooms to the sauce pan and simmer for 5 minutes.
10. Meanwhile, mix the yoghurt, 4 fresh dill sprigs in a small bowl and then add into the stew.
11. Serve with the potatoes.

PREPARE

Lunch for tomorrow: Lamb pitta

Leave some of the lamb and sauce for lunch tomorrow!

Recipes for Week 5: Day 3

BREAKFAST

Muesli with fruit

240g muesli (60g per person)
Serving of milk (soya/rice/oat or skimmed milk)
Fruit of your choice, cut into chunks (1 piece of fruit per person)

1. Place muesli in a bowl, add milk.
2. Serve with fruit.

LUNCH

Lamb pitta

4 pitta breads (1 per person)
Use some of last night's dinner including sauce

Rocket leaves, handful per person
4 tomatoes, sliced

1. Slice open the pitta bread
2. Place last night's dinner into the pitta bread with the rocket leaves and sliced tomatoes.

DINNER

Chicken with lemongrass

800g lean chicken pieces on the bone
150g sugar snap peas
16 asparagus
4 spring onions, finely sliced
Lime wedges
Brown rice

For the marinade:

1 lemongrass stalk, finely chopped
2 cloves garlic, crushed
2 teaspoons ginger, grated
2 tablespoons soy sauce
115ml chicken stock
2 teaspoons olive oil
2 tablespoons Chinese rice wine

1. Mix all the marinade ingredients in a bowl.
2. Coat the chicken thoroughly with the marinade.
3. Cover with cling film and refrigerate for up to 2 hours or overnight and, if possible, turn occasionally.
4. Preheat oven 180°C (350°F).
5. Place chicken and marinade into dish and cook for 30 minutes, turning occasionally.
6. Bring a small sauce pan to boil with water and cook asparagus and sugar snap peas for 2–3 minutes.
7. Drain and serve meat, juices and vegetables.
8. Sprinkle with spring onions and serve with brown rice and lime wedges.

NOTES

Recipes for Week 5: Day 4

Your food diary:

| Meal | Time | Description |

Breakfast:

Snacks:

Lunch:

Snacks:

Dinner:

Snacks:

BREAKFAST

Fruit porridge

240g porridge oats (60g per person)
2–3 apples, chopped
120ml of water or milk (soya/rice/oat or skimmed milk) –
   enough to cover the oats and apples

1. Slowly bring to the boil the water and/or milk in a sauce pan.
2. Add the oats and chopped apples.
3. Cook for 10 minutes, stirring continuously until thickened. If the mixture becomes too thick, add more water or milk.
4. Serve immediately.

LUNCH

Salmon salad

200g mixed salad leaves
250g cherry tomatoes, halved
Handful coriander, roughly chopped
2–3 spring onions, finely sliced
¼ cucumber, roughly chopped
4 cooked poach salmon fillets, in bite size pieces
2 yellow peppers, sliced

For the dressing:
500g soya/plain yoghurt
2 tablespoons coriander, chopped
1 garlic clove, finely chopped
4 teaspoons lemon juice
1 teaspoon ground cumin

1. Place all ingredients in a bowl and mix well, season with black pepper.
2. Cover and refrigerate for 5–10 minutes before using. If the sauce is too thick, add some water to thin it.
3. Place salad leaves, cherry tomatoes, coriander, spring onions, salmon, cucumber and yellow peppers in a salad bowl and toss.
4. Serve the salad and salmon fillets and pour dressing over the dressing.

DINNER

Fillet of beef

800g beef fillet
3 onions, finely sliced
2 teaspoons olive oil
2 teaspoons balsamic vinegar

8 mushrooms, peeled and stems removed
115ml white wine
100g fresh mixed salad leaves

1. Preheat oven to 180°C (350°F).
2. Cook the onions in olive oil, over medium heat for 20–25 minutes, or until soft. Add the balsamic vinegar and cook for a further 5 minutes.
3. Heat a non stick frying pan over high heat. Sear fillet on both sides and transfer beef to a baking dish.
4. Place mushrooms in second baking tray, pour over the wine and cover with foil.
5. Place both dishes in the oven and cook for 15 minutes.
6. Remove the beef from oven, cover with foil and leave to rest for 10 minutes.
7. At the same time, remove the foil from the mushrooms and bake for a further 10 minutes.
8. Divide the meat into 4 portions, serve with mixed salad leaves and caramelised onions and mushrooms.

PREPARE

Lunch for tomorrow: Chicken wrap

1. Heat ½ tablespoon extra virgin olive oil in a frying pan over a medium heat.
2. Cook 4 chicken breasts for 8–12 minutes, or until cooked.

BREAKFAST

LUNCH

DINNER

NOTES

Recipes for Week 5: Day 5

Your food diary:

Meal   Time   Description

Breakfast:

Snacks:

Lunch:

Snacks:

Dinner:

Snacks:

Fresh fruit and seeds

8 tablespoons of soya/plain yoghurt
Sprinkle of sunflower or pumpkin seeds
2 pieces of fruit of your choice per person

1.   Mix together the soya/plain yoghurt, seeds and fruit
2.   Divide into 4 portions.

Chicken wrap

4 cooked chicken breasts, cut into strips
4 tortilla organic whole wheat wraps (served hot or cold)
200g mixed salad
4–5 sliced tomatoes

1 red onion, finely chopped
1 yellow pepper, sliced
2 tablespoons of soya/plain yoghurt

1.   Heat ½ tablespoon extra virgin olive oil in a frying pan over a medium heat.
2.   Cook 4 chicken breasts for 8–12 minutes or until cooked.
3.   Place mixed salad, red onion, yellow pepper, tomatoes and chicken in salad bowl and mix well.
4.   Place tortilla wraps on plates, add mixture from salad bowl and roll wrap.
5.   Drizzle over the yoghurt.

Barramundi curry

1 tablespoon olive oil
800g barramundi fillet, diced
1 teaspoon sugar
115ml chicken stock
1 tablespoon fish sauce
200g runner beans
Handful of coriander
Serve with rice or vegetables

For the curry paste:
1 red chilli, roughly chopped
1 lemongrass stalk, finely chopped
2 spring onions, finely chopped
1 clove garlic, roughly chopped
2 teaspoons finely grated ginger
2 teaspoons coriander
1 teaspoon of prawn paste

1.   Place all curry paste ingredients in food processor and blend to a fine paste.
2.   Boil the rice and under a medium heat, grill the vegetables.
3.   Heat olive oil in large non-stick frying pan over medium heat.
4.   Add the curry paste and fish and stir fry for 3 minutes, turning fish carefully to coat with paste.
5.   Add the sugar, chicken stock, fish sauce and beans.
6.   Cook for a further 5 minutes.
7.   Remove from heat, sprinkle with coriander and serve.

Recipes for Week 5: Day 6

BREAKFAST

Omelette

8 eggs (2 eggs per person)
4 tablespoons water
8 teaspoons olive oil
400g lean ham
1 courgette, finely sliced
4 spring onions, finely chopped
Parsley to garnish

1. Cook omelette for one person at a time. Beat the eggs with water in a bowl.
2. Heat the olive oil in a non stick pan over a high heat.
3. Pour in eggs and cook for 2 minutes or until mixture just begins to set.
4. Place ham and courgette on top of the egg mixture and cook until omelette has set.
5. Sprinkle on parsley and spring onions.
6. Fold omelette in half and serve. Repeat process.

LUNCH

Beef and beetroot salad

4 cooked beetroots
50g parmesan, shaved
400g of lean finely sliced cold roast beef
Generous amount of salad & baby spinach
Basil, small handful of chopped

For the dressing:

1 tablespoon balsamic vinegar
2 tablespoons olive oil, cold pressed
1 clove of garlic, chopped
1 teaspoon dijon mustard

1. Add all dressing ingredients into bowl and whisk well.
2. Add the remaining ingredients into large salad bowl, and mix together.
3. Pour dressing over the top.

DINNER

Paella

60ml boiling water
2 tablespoons olive oil
1 onion finely chopped
3 tomatoes, roughly chopped
200g short grain rice
1 litre of chicken stock
400g fish of your choice
150g uncooked prawns, peeled
200g mussels, bearded and washed

150g calamari
150g peas
Spices and herbs:
1 teaspoon saffron
1 teaspoon paprika
2 cloves garlic, crushed
Small handful parsley, roughly chopped
Ground black pepper
Lemon wedges

1. In a small non stick frying pan, lightly toss saffron and transfer to a cup.
2. Crush and add paprika and 60ml of boiling water. Stir to dissolve and set aside.
3. Heat olive oil in large pan over medium heat.
4. Add the garlic and onion and cook for 5 minutes, or until soft.
5. Add the tomatoes and cook for a further 3 minutes.
6. Add rice and cook for 5 minutes, stirring continuously. Meanwhile bringing the stock to a boil in a large saucepan.
7. Add the stock and saffron liquid to the rice mixture, stir well and simmer for 15 minutes.
8. Add fish, prawns, mussels and calamari on top of rice, cover with foil and cook for 10 minutes.
9. Add peas, re-cover pan and cook for a further 5 minutes.
10. Sprinkle with parsley, season with pepper and serve with lemon wedges.

Recipes for Week 5: Day 7

Your food diary:

Meal	Time	Description
Breakfast:		
Snacks:		
Lunch:		
Snacks:		
Dinner:		
Snacks:		

Fruit smoothie

4 tablespoons nut and seed muesli
1200ml milk (soya/rice/oat or skimmed milk)
2 bananas
2 apricots
2 peaches

1. Mix the muesli and milk in a blender until nearly smooth.
2. Add the bananas, peaches and apricots and blend until completely smooth.
3. If the smoothie is too thick, add more water.

Vegetable soup

1 litre vegetable stock
2 carrots, sliced
2 celery sticks, chopped
1 onion, chopped

1 tablespoon parsley, chopped
1 x 400g tin tomatoes
1 tablespoon basil, chopped
1 tablespoon rosemary, fresh finely chopped

1. Bring stock to a boil in a large saucepan.
2. Add the carrot, celery, onion, parsley and tomatoes and simmer gently for 30 minutes.
3. Stir through basil and rosemary and season with black pepper.

Roasted chicken

1 tablespoon olive oil
1.5kg lean chicken
1 onion, peeled and roughly chopped
2 garlic cloves, peeled and finely chopped
2 celery stalks, cut into chunks
2 large carrots, cut into chunks
12 new potatoes
1 tablespoon fresh thyme

2 bay leaves
400g tinned chopped tomatoes
1 tablespoon Worcestershire sauce
300ml chicken stock
125g frozen broad beans
125g frozen peas
250g broccoli florets
Freshly ground black pepper

1. Preheat oven 190°C (375°F).
2. Heat the olive oil in a ovenproof dish, remove any excess fat and set the chicken, breast side up in the dish.
3. Add the onion, garlic, celery, carrots, potatoes, thyme and bay leaves.
4. Pour in chopped tomatoes, Worcestershire sauce and stock. Mix together and bring to a simmer.
5. Cover and cook for 1 hour or until chicken is cooked.
6. Carefully remove chicken from casserole dish.
7. Add the frozen peas, broad beans and broccoli, season with pepper and cook for 10 minutes.
8. Carve and serve vegetables with tomato sauce.

Lunch for tomorrow: Tomato chicken salad

Save some of the chicken and tomato sauce for tomorrow's lunch.

enjoy your food
week 6

Week 6 Overview

DAY	BREAKFAST	LUNCH	DINNER
1	Fruit porridge	Tomato chicken salad.	Spicy prawns
2	Wheat biscuits/Shredded Wheat or muesli with a piece of fruit	Vegetable soup	Greek chicken salad
3	Muesli with fresh fruit	Chicken wrap	Lamb with rosemary and garlic
4	Fruit smoothie	Tuna salad	Butternut squash and spinach frittata
5	Fresh fruit and seeds	Turkey and pine nut salad	Green fish curry
6	Omelette	Rice and salad with beetroot	Beef in black bean sauce
7	Fruit salad	Butternut squash and coriander soup	Kedgeree

Snack list

- **Fruits:**

  Melon, mango or coconut – 1 to share

  Peach, plum, or kiwi – 1

  Pineapple – 1 to share (I had 2 slices a week)

  Orange or nectarine – 1

  Berries (blackberries, goji, blueberries, raspberries or strawberries) – 2 portions

  Pear – 1

  Banana – 5

  Apple – 5

- **Dr Karg crackers** – 3

- **Crackers/flat breads** – 1

- **Small bowl of muesli** (if really hungry) – 2

- **Yoghurt/soya yoghurt** (four dessert spoons) – 1

- **Nuts** (cashew, pine or occasionally mixed nuts) – 2 to 3 handfuls

- **Soya nuts** – after all training sessions 3 to 4 handfuls

- **Seeds** (pumpkin or sunflower) – 2 to 3 handfuls

- **Pitta bread/wrap with salad and protein filling** – 1

I would roughly snack four to five times a day at random intervals. On average however, I snacked at 10.00am, 12.00pm, 2.30pm and 4.00pm. You can use this as a guide, but you do not need to snack five times a day – just when you need to.

Shopping List
Week 6

Carbohydrates:

1 bag of black beans
1 bag of brown basmati rice
1 bag of brown rice
1 bag of wild rice
1 tin of chickpeas
1 bag of long grain rice
250g of Jordans muesli
320g porridge oats
1 bag of rice noodles
1 bag of sunflower seeds
1 bag of pumpkin seeds
4 organic tortilla wraps
1 bag of pine nuts
8 baked potatoes
4 sweet potatoes
4 organic tortilla wraps
225g water chestnuts
12 wholemeal/brown pitta breads
Wheat biscuits/Shredded wheat

Dairy and non-dairy alternatives:

200g feta/goat's cheese
50g goat's cheese
1.88 litres skimmed/Alpro soya/ rice /oat milk
2kg Alpro soya yoghurt

Fish:

225g haddock fillets
225g smoked haddock fillets
700g cooked prawns
1.15kg tuna steaks
4 tinned tuna cans
225g x 4 white fish

Meat:

400g rump beef
8 chicken breasts
1 large whole chicken
400g lean ham
1.5kg leg of lamb
4 turkey breasts

Fruit:

7 apples
2 apricots
6 bananas
1 punnet of blackberries
1 punnet of blueberries
4 lemons
4 peaches
1 large pineapple
1 punnet of raspberries

Vegetables:

115g baby corn
300g baby spinach
4 cooked beetroot
12 black olives
225g broccoli
1.4kg butternut squash
6 cherry tomatoes
4 carrots
4 celery sticks
1 cos lettuce
1 courgette
1½ cucumber
2 leeks
2 lettuce
50g mange tout
3 onions
8 plum tomatoes
2 red onions
2 red peppers
4 red tomatoes
175g rocket salad
4 shallots
20 spring onions
1 turnip
1 yellow pepper

Fruit drinks

1 carton Tropicana/Innocent fruit drink

Herbs:

Basil
Black pepper
Chilli powder
Coriander
Ground coriander
Coriander seeds
Fresh ginger
2 green chillies
1 garlic clove
Mint
Nutmeg
Paprika
Parsley
4 red chillies
Rosemary
Turmeric

Other:

Balsamic vinegar
Brown sugar
150ml coconut milk
Chicken stock
Chinese rice vinegar
Cold pressed extra virgin olive oil
Peanut oil
Soy sauce
Tahini
400g tinned tomatoes
Vegetable stock
115ml white wine

Snacks:

Fruit
Dr Karg crackers
Crackers/flat breads
Small bowl of muesli
Yoghurt/Alpro soya yoghurt
Nuts (cashew, pine or occasionally mixed nuts)
Soya nuts
Seeds (pumpkin or sunflower)

Recipes for Week 6: Day 1

BREAKFAST

Fruit porridge

240g of porridge oats (60g per person)

2–3 apples, chopped

120ml of water or milk (soya/rice/oat or skimmed milk) –
enough to cover the oats and apples

1. Slowly bring to the boil the water and/or milk in a sauce pan.
2. Add the oats and chopped apples.
3. Cook for 10 minutes, stirring continuously until thickened. If the mixture becomes too thick, add more water or milk.
4. Serve immediately.

LUNCH

Tomato chicken salad

Cooked chicken from previous night, cut into pieces

Generous amount of salad leaves

1 red pepper, sliced

1 yellow pepper, sliced

2 spring onions, finely chopped

1. Prepare the salad and place chicken over the top.
2. Serve immediately.

DINNER

Spicy prawns

2 garlic cloves, finely chopped

2cm piece of fresh ginger, thinly sliced

4 fresh red chillies, deseeded and finely chopped

Olive oil, 1 tablespoon

4 spring onions, chopped

Serve with rice and vegetables of your choice

2 green peppers, deseeded and sliced

400g tin tomatoes

½ tablespoon brown sugar

700g cooked prawns, peel

4 spring onions, finely sliced to garnish

1. Heat the olive oil in a large wok or frying pan over medium heat.
2. Add ginger, chilli and garlic, stir constantly for 1 minute – do not brown.
3. Add the spring onions and green peppers stir for 5 minutes.
4. Next, add the tinned tomatoes and sugar, bring to boil and stir constantly. If sauce is too thick, add a little water.
5. Reduce heat and simmer for 5 minutes.
6. Stir in the prawns and cook for 4 minutes.
7. Transfer food to plates, garnish with spring onions and serve.

PREPARE

Lunch for tomorrow: Vegetable soup

1. Bring stock to boil in a large saucepan.
2. Add the carrot, celery, onion, parsley and tomatoes and simmer gently for 30 minutes.
3. Stir through basil and rosemary and season with black pepper and allow to cool.
4. Refrigerate for tomorrow's lunch.

Recipes for Week 6: Day 2

BREAKFAST

Wheat biscuits, Shredded Wheat or muesli with a fruit

560ml milk (soya/rice/oat or skimmed milk)
2–3 wheat biscuits/Shredded Wheat or 240g of muesli, (60g per person)
1 piece of fruit of your choice

Place oats or cereal in a bowl add milk and serve with fruit.

LUNCH

Vegetable soup

1 litre vegetable stock
2 carrots, sliced
2 celery sticks, chopped
1 onion, chopped

1 tablespoon fresh parsley, chopped
400g tin tomatoes
1 tablespoon basil, chopped
1 tablespoon rosemary, finely chopped

1. Bring stock to boil in a large saucepan.
2. Add the carrots, celery, onion, parsley and tomatoes and simmer gently for 30 minutes.
3. Stir through basil and rosemary and season with black pepper.

DINNER

Greek chicken salad

1 cos lettuce, cut into large pieces
1 cucumber, roughly chopped
1 green pepper, deseeded and finely chopped
12 olives (optional)
½ red onion, finely sliced
8 plum tomatoes
1 tablespoon lemon juice
1 tablespoon olive oil
200g low fat feta/goat's cheese
4 chicken breasts
8 wholemeal pitta breads (2 per person)

For the tzatziki:
1 clove of garlic, crushed
200g soya/plain yoghurt
¼ cucumber, finely grated
½ small red onion, finely chopped
1 tablespoon parsley, chopped
1 tablespoon mint, chopped
For the humous:
1 large tin chickpeas, drained
2 cloves garlic, peeled
2–3 tablespoons olive oil
1 dessertspoon tahini (sesame seed spread)

1. Put the lettuce, cucumber, pepper, olives, tomatoes and onion into a large salad bowl.
2. Add the olive oil and lemon juice and mix well.
3. Crumble the feta/goat's cheese or mature goat's cheese cheese over the top.
4. Prepare the tzatziki by mixing all the ingredients together in a small bowl.
5. Prepare humous by placing all the ingredients in a blender and blend until a smooth paste.
6. Meanwhile, grill the chicken on a medium heat for 8–12 minutes, or until thoroughly cooked.
7. Allow to cool for a couple of minutes and cut into pieces.
8. Toast the pitta bread before serving then fill with chicken, salad, tzatziki and humous. Save some tzatziki for lunch tomorrow!

PREPARE

Lunch for tomorrow: Chicken wrap

1. Cook 4 chicken breasts (1 per person) for tomorrow's lunch.
2. Heat ½ tablespoon extra virgin olive oil in a frying pan over a medium heat.
3. Cook the chicken for 8–12 minutes, or until cooked.

Your food diary:

Meal	Time	Description
Breakfast:		
Snacks:		
Lunch:		
Snacks:		
Dinner:		
Snacks:		

Your food diary:

Meal   Time   Description

Breakfast:

Snacks:

Lunch:

Snacks:

Dinner:

Snacks:

Recipes for Week 6: Day 3

BREAKFAST

Muesli with fresh fruit

240g muesli (60g per person)
Serving of milk (soya/rice/oat or skimmed milk)
Fruit of your choice, cut into chunks (1 piece of fruit per person)

1. Place muesli in a bowl, add milk.
2. Serve with fruit.

LUNCH

Chicken wrap

4 cooked chicken breasts, cut into strips
4 tortilla organic whole wheat wraps (served hot or cold)
200g mixed salad
4–5 sliced tomatoes

1 red onion, finely chopped
1 yellow pepper, sliced
2 tablespoons of soya/plain yoghurt

1. Heat ½ tablespoon extra virgin olive oil in a frying pan over a medium heat.
2. Cook 4 chicken breasts for 8–12 minutes or until cooked.
3. Place mixed salad, red onion, yellow pepper, tomatoes and chicken in salad bowl and mix well.
4. Place tortilla wraps on plates, add mixture from salad bowl and roll wrap.
5. Drizzle over the yoghurt.

DINNER

Lamb with rosemary and garlic

1.5kg lean leg of lamb (200g per person)
1 tablespoon olive oil
2 sprigs rosemary
2 cloves garlic, peeled and halved

2 lemons quartered
115ml white wine
Serve with your favourite vegetables or beans
and 8 roast potatoes (2 per person)

1. Preheat oven to 180°C (350°F).
2. Rub meat with olive oil.
3. Place rosemary, garlic and lemon in a baking dish and pour in the white wine.
4. Add lamb on top and bake for 1 to 1½ hours depending on taste.
5. Cook your vegetables and roast the potatoes.
6. Remove from oven, cover with foil and set aside for 10 minutes before carving.

PREPARE

Lunch for tomorrow: Tuna salad

1. Preheat oven 190°C (375°F).
2. Cut the sweet potatoes into small chunks and drizzle a tablespoon of exra virgin olive oil.
3. Place in oven for 30–40 minutes.
4. Once cooked allow to cool then refridgerate for tommorow's lunch.

Recipes for Week 6: Day 4

BREAKFAST

Fruit smoothie

4 tablespoons nut and seed muesli
1200ml milk (soya/rice/oat or skimmed milk)
2 bananas
2 apricots
2 peaches

1. Mix the muesli and milk in a blender until nearly smooth.
2. Add the bananas, peaches and apricots and blend until completely smooth.
3. If the smoothie is too thick, add more water.

LUNCH

Tuna salad

4 cooked sweet potatoes
4 small tinned tuna
1 tablespoon balsamic vinegar
1 tablespoon olive oil

Side salad:
100g of rocket leaves
4 tomatoes, roughly chopped
¼ cucumber, roughly chopped
50g mange-tout
1 red pepper, sliced

1. Preheat oven 190C (375°F). Cut the sweet potatoes into small chunks and drizzle a tablespoon of exra virgin olive oil and place into oven for 30–40 minutes.
2. Once cooked, allow to cool and place into the fridge for tommorrow's lunch.
3. Place rocket leaves, mange-tout, tomatoes, cucumber and red pepper in a salad bowl and gently mix with balsamic vinegar and olive.
4. Serve with the tuna and sweet potatoes.

DINNER

Butternut squash and spinach frittata

400g butternut squash, peeled and cut into 3cm cubes
1 tablespoon olive oil
1 teaspoon soy sauce
2 leeks, finely chopped and washed
2 cloves garlic, crushed

300g baby spinach
8 eggs
400g soya/plain yoghurt
50g matured/goat's cheese, grated
Serve with salad

1. Preheat oven to 170°C (330°F). Grease a small baking dish with a little olive oil.
2. Place butternut squash in baking tray, add 1 teaspoon of olive oil and soy sauce, roast for 25 minutes.
3. Heat the rest of the olive oil over medium heat.
4. Add the leek and cook for 5 minutes, or until soft. Then add the garlic and spinach leaves and cook until spinach has wilted.
5. Whisk eggs, soya/plain yoghurt and cheese together in large bowl.
6. Then add the butternut squash and spinach mixture and gently stir.
7. Pour the mixture into a baking dish and cook for 20 minutes, or until set.
8. Serve with a salad.

PREPARE

Lunch for tomorrow: Turkey and pine nut salad

1. Heat ½ tablespoon extra virgin olive oil in a frying pan over a medium heat.
2. Cook the 4 turkey breasts for 8–12 minutes, or until cooked.
3. Allow to cool then refrigerate overnight.

Recipes for Week 6: Day 5

Your food diary:

Meal	Time	Description
Breakfast:		
Snacks:		
Lunch:		
Snacks:		
Dinner:		
Snacks:		

Fresh fruit and seeds

8 tablespoons of soya/plain yoghurt
Sprinkle of sunflower or pumpkin seeds
2 pieces of fruit of your choice per person

1. Mix together the yoghurt, seeds and fruit
2. Divide into 4 portions.

Turkey and pine nut salad

3–4 tablespoons pine nuts
4 cooked turkey breast, cut into pieces
Generous amount of salad leaves
1 avocado, sliced

1 red pepper, sliced
1 yellow pepper, sliced
2 spring onions, finely chopped

1. Prepare the salad and arrange the cooked turkey on top of the leaves.
2. Sprinkle with the pine nuts.
3. Drizzle over balsamic vinegar and serve immediately.

Green fish curry

1 tablespoon olive oil
2 spring onions, sliced
1 teaspoon ground cumin seeds
2 green chillies, finely chopped
1 teaspoon coriander seeds
Serve with basmati rice and vegetables of your choice

4 tablespoons fresh coriander
4 tablespoons fresh mint
150ml/5 fl oz coconut milk
4 white fish fillets (225g/8oz each)

1. Heat the olive oil in large frying pan over medium heat. Add the spring onions and cook for 2 minutes or until soft.
2. Stir in ground cumin, chillies and coriander seeds and cook until the spices are fragrant.
3. Add the fresh coriander, mint, and coconut milk.
4. Carefully cook fish in frying pan 10–15 minutes or until the flesh flakes easily when tested with a fork.
5. Transfer the fish onto plates and serve with rice and vegetables of your choice.
6. Garnish with fresh mint and enjoy!

Dinner for tomorrow: Beef in black bean sauce

For the marinade:

1 tablespoon black beans,
  soaked in cold water for 5–10 minutes
2 tablespoons dark soy sauce
2 tablespoons Chinese rice wine

1 tablespoon peanut oil
1 teaspoon brown sugar
1 garlic clove, thinly sliced
1 tablespoon ginger, finely chopped

1. To make marinade, mash black beans in bowl with fork gently stir in remaining marinade ingredients and blend with a food processor.
2. Pour the marinade over steak.
3. Cover and refrigerate over night.

Recipes for Week 6: Day 6

BREAKFAST

Omelette

8 eggs (2 eggs per person)
4 tablespoons cold water
8 teaspoons olive oil
400g lean ham
1 courgette, finely sliced
4 spring onions, finely chopped
Parsley to garnish

1. Cook omelette for one person at a time. Beat the eggs with water in a bowl.
2. Heat the olive oil in a non stick pan over a high heat.
3. Pour in eggs and cook for 2 minutes or until mixture just begins to set.
4. Place ham and courgette on top of the egg mixture and cook until omelette has set.
5. Sprinkle on parsley and spring onions. Fold omelette in half and serve. Repeat process.

LUNCH

Rice and salad with beetroot

100g brown rice
100g wild rice
4 shallots, peeled and halved
2 teaspoons olive oil

4 cooked beetroots, finely diced
1 lemon, juice of
2 tablespoons fresh mint, chopped
2 tablespoons fresh parsley, chopped

1. Preheat oven to 200°C (400°F). Place brown and wild rice in medium sauce pan of water, bring to boil and simmer for 20 minutes.
2. Place the shallots on a baking tray and drizzle with olive oil and roast for 8–10 minutes.
3. Drain the rice and allow to cool. Mix the beetroot, lemon juice and mint. Stir in shallots and parsley then serve.

DINNER

Beef in black bean sauce

400g lean rump steak, remove fat, cut into chunks
1 tablespoon olive oil
225g broccoli, cut into florets
115g baby corns, cut in half
4 spring onions, sliced diagonally
225g tinned water chestnuts
Rice noodles/ egg noodles

For the marinade:

1 tablespoon black beans,
 soaked in cold water for 5–10 minutes
2 tablespoons dark soy sauce
2 tablespoons Chinese rice wine
1 tablespoon peanut oil
1 teaspoon brown sugar
1 garlic clove, thinly sliced
1 tablespoon ginger, finely chopped

1. To make marinade: mash black beans in a bowl with a fork and stir in the remaining marinade ingredients and blend with a food processor.
2. Pour the marinade over steak and coat thoroughly in a baking dish. Cover with cling film and leave in fridge for 6 + hours.
3. Heat the olive oil in large wok or frying pan. Drain the steak and reserve the marinade.
4. Stir fry the steak over a medium/high heat for 3 minutes, then transfer to a plate.
5. Add the broccoli and baby corn cobs to the wok and stir in 3 tablespoons of water, cover and steam for 5 minutes, or until the vegetables are tender.
6. Add spring onions and water chestnuts to the wok and stir fry for a further 2 minutes.
7. Return the steak to the wok and pour in the reserved marinade.
8. Cook and keep stirring, until heated through. Serve with noodles of your choice.

Your food diary:

Meal	Time	Description
Breakfast:		
Snacks:		
Lunch:		
Snacks:		
Dinner:		
Snacks:		

BREAKFAST

LUNCH

DINNER

Recipes for Week 6: Day 7

Your food diary:

Meal	Time	Description

Breakfast:

Snacks:

Lunch:

Snacks:

Dinner:

Snacks:

Fruit salad

8 tablespoons soya/plain yoghurt (2 tablespoons per person)

80g oats

60g sunflower seeds or pumpkin seeds

4–5 pieces of fruit (preferably ones in season)

1. Dice fruit into chunks and divide into 4 portions.
2. Add 2 tablespoons of yoghurt in each portion and sprinkle with oats and seeds.

Butternut squash and coriander soup

900ml chicken stock

1kg butternut squash, peeled and chopped

1 onion, roughly chopped

2 carrots, roughly chopped

2 celery sticks, roughly chopped

1 garlic clove, finely chopped

1 teaspoon paprika

½ teaspoon turmeric

½ teaspoon ground coriander

½ teaspoon ground nutmeg

1. In a large saucepan, bring chicken stock to boil.
2. Add vegetables and spices and bring back to boil.
3. Reduce heat and simmer for 20 minutes, or until vegetables are soft.
4. Allow to cool and then blend.
5. Reheat soup and serve.

Kedgeree

225g haddock fillets

225g smoked haddock fillet

1 tablespoon olive oil

1 onion, chopped

225g long grain rice

1 hard boiled egg, cut into quarters

2 tablespoons fresh parsley

Spices:

½ teaspoon ground turmeric

½ teaspoon cumin

½ teaspoon chilli powder

¼ teaspoon ground ginger

1. Place the haddock and smoked haddock in large frying pan.
2. Pour enough water to cover and poach gently over a low heat for 10–15 minutes.
3. Remove from heat and allow to cool.
4. Sieve the cooking liquid into a measuring jug and make it up to 600ml if necessary.
5. Heat the olive oil in a large frying pan.
6. Add the onions and cook on low heat for 3 minutes, or until soft.
7. Mix in the spices, add the rice and cook. Stir until well coated.
8. Gently stir in the reserved liquid and bring to boil.
9. Cover and cook over low heat for 20 minutes, or until the liquid has been absorbed into the rice.
10. Meanwhile, skin the fish and remove any remaining bones.
11. Flake the flesh and fold the fish into rice.
12. Transfer to a serving dish and garnish with a boiled egg.
13. Sprinkle over the chopped parsley and serve immediately.

enjoy your food
week 7

Week 7 Overview

DAY	BREAKFAST	LUNCH	DINNER
1	Wheat biscuits/Shredded Wheat or muesli with a piece of fruit	Beef salad pitta	Snapper with basil
2	Fruit salad	Yellow split pea soup	Chicken with roasted tomatoes
3	Muesli and fresh fruit	Chicken wrap	Lamb with baked fennel
4	Fruit porridge	Egg salad	Citrus baked cod
5	Fresh fruit and seeds	Tuna salad	Soya/plain yoghurt baked chicken
6	Omelette	Tomato and pepper soup.	Vegetarian stir fry
7	Fruit smoothie	Salmon salad	Spiced barramundi fillets

Snack list

- **Fruits:**

  Melon, mango or coconut – 1 to share

  Peach, plum, or kiwi – 1

  Pineapple – 1 to share (I had 2 slices a week)

  Orange or nectarine – 1

  Berries (blackberries, goji, blueberries, raspberries or strawberries) – 2 portions

  Pear – 1

  Banana – 5

  Apple – 5
- **Dr Karg crackers** – 3
- **Crackers/flat breads** – 1
- **Small bowl of muesli** (if really hungry) – 2
- **Yoghurt/soya yoghurt** (four dessert spoons) – 1
- **Nuts** (cashew, pine or occasionally mixed nuts) – 2 to 3 handfuls
- **Soya nuts** – after all training sessions 3 to 4 handfuls
- **Seeds** (pumpkin or sunflower) – 2 to 3 handfuls
- **Pitta bread/wrap with salad and protein filling** – 1

I would roughly snack four to five times a day at random intervals. On average however, I snacked at 10.00am, 12.00pm, 2.30pm and 4.00pm. You can use this as a guide, but you do not need to snack five times a day – just when you need to.

Shopping List
Week 7

Carbohydrates:

1 bag of brown rice
12 charlotte potatoes
240g of Jordans muesli
560g porridge oats
1 bag of rice noodles
1 bag of sunflower
1 bag of pumpkin seeds
4 organic tortilla wraps
1 bag of sesame seeds
5 sweet potatoes
4 wholemeal/brown pitta breads
225g yellow split peas
Wheat biscuits/Shredded wheat

Dairy and non-dairy alternatives:

12 eggs
60g feta/goat's cheese
680ml skimmed/Alpro soya/rice
   /oat milk
2kg Alpro soya yoghurt

Fish:

200g x 4 barramundi
175g x 4 cod/hake
200g x 4 snapper fillets
4 poached salmon fillets
4 tins tuna

Meat:

400g cooked roast beef
12 chicken breasts
400g lean ham
1.4kg lamb cutlets

Fruit:

3 apples
4 bananas
2 lemons
2 limes
2 mangos
1 melon
1 orange
1 large pineapple
1 punnet of raspberries

Vegetables:

100g baby corn
3 bags of baby spinach
55g button mushrooms
1 broccoli floret
350g cabbage
400g cherry tomatoes
3 carrots
1 courgette
1½ cucumbers
2 fennel bulbs
1 green pepper
4 lettuce
200g mange tout
150g mushrooms
5 onions
5 red onions
4 red peppers
100g rocket salad
200g savoy cabbage
230g snow pea pods
11 spring onions
5 yellow peppers

Fruit drinks

1 carton Tropicana/Innocent fruit
drink

Herbs:

Basil
Black pepper
Cardamom seeds
Chilli powder
Chinese five spice
Cinnamon
Coriander
Cumin
Fresh ginger
1 garlic clove
Mint
Oregano
Parsley
1 red chilli
Rosemary
Tarragon

Other:

Balsamic vinegar
Cider vinegar
Cold pressed extra virgin olive oil
Dijon mustard
Oyster stock
Peanut oil
Sesame oil
Soy sauce
Tomato puree
Vegetable stock
60ml white wine

Snacks:

Fruits:
Dr Karg crackers
Crackers/flat breads
Small bowl of muesli
Yoghurt/Alpro soya yoghurt
Nuts (cashew, pine or
   occasionally mixed nuts)
Soya nuts
Seeds (pumpkin or sunflower)

Recipes for Week 7: Day 1

BREAKFAST

Wheat biscuits, Shredded Wheat or muesli with a fruit

560ml milk (soya/rice/oat or skimmed milk)
2–3 wheat biscuits/Shredded Wheat or 240g of muesli, (60g per person)
1 piece of fruit of your choice

Place oats or cereal in a bowl add milk and serve with fruit.

LUNCH

Beef salad pitta

4 wholemeal pitta breads, hot or cold
400g cold roast beef, finely sliced
Generous amounts of green salad
   (cos lettuce, rocket, baby spinach, etc)
4 large tomatoes, sliced
1 red pepper, sliced
½ a small red onion, finely sliced
2 tablespoons basil, chopped

For the dressing:
2 tablespoons olive oil
1 tablespoon balsamic vinegar
1 clove garlic, crushed
1 teaspoon dijon mustard
Season with black pepper

1. In a small bowl, mix all the dressing ingredients.
2. Put the remaining ingredients in a large salad bowl and toss.
3. Slice open the pitta bread and fill with beef and salad.
4. Pour the dressing over the top and serve.

DINNER

Snapper with basil

4 x 200g snapper fillets
2 tablespoons olive oil
1 clove garlic, crushed
½ red chilli, finely chopped
4 spring onions, finely chopped

2 tablespoons basil, roughly chopped
1 tablespoon dried oregano
60ml white wine
4 tomatoes, roughly chopped
Serve with green salad

1. Preheat oven to 180°C (350°F).
2. Heat half the olive oil in a small saucepan over a medium heat.
3. Add the chilli, garlic and spring onions and stir fry for 2 minutes, or until garlic is golden.
4. Reduce the heat to medium low and add the herbs and white wine, stirring occasionally for 5 minutes.
5. Remove from heat and stir in the chopped tomatoes.
6. Heat a large non-stick frying pan over a high heat and brush the fish with the remaining oil.
7. Sear each side for 2 minutes and transfer to an ovenproof baking dish and spoon sauce over fish.
8. Bake for 6–8 minutes or until fish is cooked. The flesh will flake away easily when pressed with a fork when the fish is ready and serve with salad.

PREPARE

Lunch for tomorrow: Yellow split pea soup

Soak the yellow split peas for tomorrow's lunch.

Recipes for Week 7: Day 2

Your food diary:

Meal	Time	Description
Breakfast:		
Snacks:		
Lunch:		
Snacks:		
Dinner:		
Snacks:		

Fruit salad

8 tablespoons soya/plain yoghurt (2 tablespoons per person)
80g oats
60g sunflower seeds or pumpkin seeds
4-5 pieces of fruit (preferably ones in season)

1. Dice fruit into chunks and divide into 4 portions.
2. Add 2 tablespoons of yoghurt in each portion and sprinkle with oats and seeds.

Yellow split pea soup

225g yellow split peas
  (Pre-soak for 12 hours overnight in cold water)
1.5 litres of vegetable stock
1 onion, peeled and sliced

1 sweet potato, peeled and chopped
3 carrots, trimmed, peeled and sliced
Fresh mint
Fresh baby spinach leaves, 4 handfuls

1. Drain water from the split peas.
2. Bring the vegetable stock to boil in a large saucepan and add split peas.
3. Simmer for 25 minutes removing any scum on the surface.
4. Add all other vegetables to the saucepan and simmer for a further 15–20 minutes or until vegetables are tender.
5. Remove from heat and allow too cool.
6. Blend soup with food processor or blender.
7. Reheat soup and add the spinach.
8. Serve with a mint garnish.

Chicken with roasted tomatoes

4 large tomatoes, cut into quarters
1 tablespoon olive oil
1 small onion, sliced
1 tablespoon fresh basil, roughly chopped

4 x 200g skinless chicken breasts
60g goat's or mature cheese, cut into chunks
Serve with salad and vegetables of your choice

1. Preheat oven to 180°C (350°F). Line a baking tray with baking paper and place tomatoes on tray.
2. Place in a hot oven for 15 minutes. Meanwhile, heat the olive oil in a frying pan over medium heat.
3. Add in the onion and basil and cook for 5 minutes or until onion is soft.
4. Drain and reserve the oil and place onion and basil on a plate.
5. Return pan to heat and add the reserved oil.
6. Add chicken and cook for 6 minutes each side, or until lightly browned on both sides.
7. Heat grill to medium.
8. Divide the chicken into 4 portions and cover the chicken with a layer of tomato and onion mixture.
9. Top with feta/goat's cheese or mature goat's cheese/goat's cheese or mature goat's cheese and place under grill until the cheese has melted.
10. Serve with either salad or vegetables.

Lunch for tomorrow: Chicken wrap

1. Heat ½ tablespoon extra virgin olive oil in a frying pan over a medium heat.
2. Cook the chicken for 8–12 minutes or until cooked.

Recipes for Week 7: Day 3

BREAKFAST

Muesli with fresh fruit

240g muesli (60g per person)
Serving of milk (soya/rice/oat or skimmed milk)
Fruit of your choice, cut into chunks (1 piece of fruit per person)

1. Place muesli in a bowl, add milk.
2. Serve with fruit.

LUNCH

Chicken wrap

4 cooked chicken breasts, cut into strips
4 tortilla organic whole wheat wraps (served hot or cold)
200g mixed salad
4-5 sliced tomatoes

1 red onion, finely chopped
1 yellow pepper, sliced
2 tablespoons of soya/plain yoghurt

1. Heat ½ tablespoon extra virgin olive oil in a frying pan over a medium heat.
2. Cook 4 chicken breasts for 8–12 minutes or until cooked.
3. Place mixed salad, red onion, yellow pepper, tomatoes and chicken in salad bowl and mix well.
4. Place tortilla wraps on plates, add mixture from salad bowl and roll wrap.
5. Drizzle over the yoghurt.

DINNER

Lamb with baked fennel

1.4kg lamb cutlets (200g meat per person) trim off the fat
2 fennel bulbs, sliced
2 red onions, cut into wedges
1 tablespoon olive oil
100g baby spinach leaves
8 – 12 charlotte potatoes

For the marinade:

2 tablespoons rosemary, chopped
2 teaspoons tarragon, chopped
2 teaspoons parsley
1 tablespoon olive oil

1. Mix the marinade ingredients together and pour into a shallow dish.
2. Add the meat to the marinade and coat thoroughly.
3. Cover and allow marinate for 30 minutes.
4. Preheat oven to 180°C (350°F).
5. Place fennel and onion in a baking dish and drizzle with olive oil and bake for 20 minutes.
6. Roast the potatoes.
7. Preheat grill to high and cook the lamb cutlets to your liking.
8. Once cooked, set a side to rest. Toss the spinach leaves through the hot vegetables.
9. Arrange the vegetables on serving plates and place the lamb on top.
10. Serve with potatoes.

PREPARE

Lunch for tomorrow: Egg salad

1. Boil the 4 eggs for 6½ minutes
2. Place in cold water and allow to cool.
3. Refrigerate overnight.

BREAKFAST

LUNCH

DINNER

PREPARE

Recipes for Week 7: Day 4

Fruit porridge

240g of porridge oats (60g per person)
2–3 apples, chopped
120ml of water or milk (soya/rice/oat or skimmed milk) –
enough to cover the oats and apples

1. Slowly bring to the boil the water and/or milk in a sauce pan.
2. Add the oats and chopped apples.
3. Cook for 10 minutes, stirring continuously until thickened. If the mixture becomes too thick, add more water or milk.
4. Serve immediately.

Egg salad

4 baby gem lettuce
200g baby spinach
150g cherry tomatoes, halved
4 shelled hard-boiled eggs, cut into quarters
½ cucumber, sliced
1 yellow pepper, deseeded and sliced

For the dressing:
1 tablespoon dijon mustard
1 tablespoon olive oil
2 teaspoons cider vinegar
1 teaspoon water

1. Arrange the lettuce, spinach, tomatoes, yellow pepper, and cucumber on plates.
2. Mix the mustard and water add mix in the olive oil and vinegar into a small bowl.
3. Put the eggs on top of the salad, drizzle with the dressing and serve.

Citrus baked cod

4 x cod or hake cutlets (175g/6oz each)
2 tablespoons lime juice
1 green pepper, deseeded and cut into strips
1 tablespoon olive oil
1 onion, finely chopped
1 clove garlic, crushed

40g/1.5oz pumpkin seeds
1 lime, grated rind
1 tablespoon coriander, chopped
55g/2oz button mushrooms, finely sliced
2 tablespoons fresh orange juice or white wine
Serve with steamed broccoli

1. Place fish in a shallow ovenproof dish and pour over lime juice.
2. Cover and leave to marinade in the refrigerator for 15–25 minutes.
3. Preheat oven to 180°C (350°F).
4. Heat olive oil in a frying pan and cook onion, garlic, green pepper and pumpkin seeds. Cook until onion is soft.
5. Gently stir in the lime rind, chopped coriander and mushrooms.
6. Spoon this mixture over fish and pour over the orange juice.
7. Cover and bake in oven for 30 minutes, or until fish is tender.
8. Serve with broccoli.

Lunch for tomorrow: Tuna salad

1. Preheat oven 190°C (375°F)
2. Cut the sweet potatoes into small chunks and drizzle over a tablespoon of exra virgin olive oil.
3. Place in oven for 30–40 minutes.
4. Once cooked allow to cool and refridgerate for tommorrow's lunch.

Recipes for Week 7: Day 5

Your food diary:

Meal   Time   Description

Breakfast:

Snacks:

Lunch:

Snacks:

Dinner:

Snacks:

BREAKFAST

Fresh fruit and seeds

8 tablespoons of soya/plain yoghurt
Sprinkle of sunflower or pumpkin seeds
2 pieces of fruit of your choice per person

1. Mix together the soya/plain yoghurt, seeds and fruit
2. Divide into 4 portions.

LUNCH

Tuna salad

4 cooked sweet potatoes
4 small tins tuna
1 tablespoon balsamic vinegar
1 tablespoon olive oil

Side salad:

100g of rocket leaves
4 tomatoes, roughly chopped
¼ cucumber, roughly chopped
50g mange-tout
1 red pepper, sliced

1. Preheat oven 190°C (375°F).
2. Cut the sweet potatoes into small chunks and drizzle a tablespoon of exra virgin olive oil and place into oven for 30–40 minutes.
3. Once cooked, allow to cool and place into the fridge for tommorrows lunch.
4. Place rocket leaves, mange-tout, tomatoes, cucumber and red pepper in a salad bowl and gently mix with balsamic vinegar and olive oil.
5. Serve with the tuna and sweet potatoes.

DINNER

Soya/plain yoghurt baked chicken

1 tablespoon olive oil
4 x 200g skinless chicken breasts
For the salad:
½ cucumber, sliced
4 large tomatoes, sliced
½ small red onion, finely sliced
½ tablespoon mint leaves
1 teaspoon lemon juice

For the marinade:
½ teaspoon Chinese five spice powder
1 teaspoon chilli powder
2 teaspoons soy sauce
1 glove garlic, crushed
1 tablespoon olive oil
200g soya/plain yoghurt

1. In a bowl fold the five spice powder, chilli powder, soy sauce, garlic and olive oil through the soya/plain yoghurt.
2. Coat the chicken with the mixture and leave to marinate for up to 4 hours.
3. Preheat the oven to 180°C (350°F).
4. Line a baking dish with baking paper.
5. Heat the olive oil in a non-stick frying pan over medium heat.
6. Add the chicken and cook for 2 minutes each side.
7. Transfer the chicken to the prepared baking dish and bake for 6–8 minutes or until cooked.
8. Remove from oven and allow to rest for 5 minutes.
9. Cut into thick slices.
10. Prepare the salad adding all the ingredients in salad bowl and mix.
11. Serve salad with the chicken.

Recipes for Week 7: Day 6

Your food diary:

Meal	Time	Description
Breakfast:		
Snacks:		
Lunch:		
Snacks:		
Dinner:		
Snacks:		

BREAKFAST

Omelette

8 eggs (2 eggs per person)
4 tablespoons of cold water
8 teaspoons olive oil
400g lean ham
1 courgette, finely sliced
4 spring onions, finely chopped
Parsley to garnish

1. Cook omelette for one person at a time. Beat the eggs with water in a bowl.
2. Heat the olive oil in a non stick pan over a high heat.
3. Pour in eggs and cook for 2 minutes or until mixture just begins to set.
4. Place ham and courgette on top of the egg mixture and cook until omelette has set.
5. Sprinkle on parsley and spring onions.
6. Fold omelette in half and serve. Repeat process.

LUNCH

Tomato and pepper soup

2 red peppers, deseeded and halved
2 tablespoons olive oil
1 large onion, finely sliced
2 cloves of garlic, crushed

1 tablespoon tomato paste
750g tomatoes, roughly chopped
450ml vegetable stock
Basil, handful

1. Preheat oven 180°C (350°F).
2. Place red peppers in baking tray, skin side up and drizzle with half the olive oil.
3. Roast for 25 minutes, or until soft and remove from oven. Allow to cool slightly, then roughly chop.
4. Heat the rest of the oil in a large saucepan, over medium heat.
5. Add the onion and cook until soft.
6. Add garlic and tomato paste and cook for 2 minutes, stirring continuously.
7. Add red pepper, tomato and stock, cover and simmer for 15 minutes.
8. Allow the soup to cool slightly, and gently stir.
9. Season with basil and serve.

DINNER

Vegetarian stir fry

1 tablespoon peanut oil
1 clove garlic
1 teaspoon ginger, grated
1 onion, sliced
150g mange-tout
150g mushrooms

350g cabbage, shredded
100g baby corn
2 tablespoons oyster sauce
1 tablespoon soy sauce
2 tablespoons coriander leaves
Serve with brown rice

1. Heat a large wok or frying pan over high heat.
2. Add peanut oil and once pan is smoking, add the garlic, ginger and onion.
3. Stir fry for 2–3 minutes or until the onion begins to soften.
4. Next, add the mange-tout, mushrooms, cabbage and baby corn and stir-fry for a further 5 minutes, or until almost cooked.
5. Add the oyster sauce, soy sauce and coriander and cook for 1 minute.
6. Serve immediately with brown rice.

Recipes for Week 7: Day 7

Fruit smoothie

2 large mangos, peeled and chopped

4 bananas, chopped

2 handfuls of raspberries

Blend mangos, bananas and raspberries and serve.

Salmon salad

200g mixed salad leaves

250g cherry tomatoes, halved

Handful coriander, roughly chopped

2–3 spring onions, finely sliced

¼ cucumber, roughly chopped

4 poached salmon fillets, bite size pieces

2 yellow peppers, sliced

For the dressing:

500g soya/plain yoghurt

2 tablespoons coriander, chopped

1 garlic clove, finely chopped

4 teaspoons lemon juice

1 teaspoon ground cumin

1. Place all ingredients in a bowl and mix well, season with black pepper.
2. Cover and refrigerate for 5–10 minutes before using. If the sauce is too thick, add some water to thin.
3. Place salad leaves, cherry tomatoes, coriander, spring onions, salmon, cucumber and yellow peppers in a salad bowl and toss. Serve the salad and salmon fillets and pour dressing over the dressing.

Spiced barramundi steaks

For the paste:

Freshly ground pepper

1 teaspoon ground cumin

1 teaspoon ground coriander

½ teaspoon ground cardamom

½ teaspoon ground cinnamon

1 clove garlic, chopped

1 tablespoon fresh coriander

1 tablespoon parsley

1 lemon, juice and finely grated zest

1 tablespoon olive oil

4 x 200g barramundi fillets

1 tablespoon sesame oil

½lb snow pea pods (string removed)

1 tablespoon sesame seeds

1 large yellow pepper, cut into thin strips

Serve with brown rice

1. Preheat oven to 180°C (350°F). Pat fish with paper towel, brush with half the oil and season.
2. Place fish in a single layer in an ovenproof baking dish.
3. Next, mix the remaining ingredients to a loose paste and spread evenly over the top of the fish.
4. Cover dish with foil and bake for 10–15 minutes, or until fish is cooked. Boil the rice.
5. Heat the sesame oil over medium to high heat and add the sea pods and sesame seeds.
6. Cook for 2 minutes or until sea pods are crisp tender. Gently stir in the yellow pepper and cook for a further 2 minutes. Serve immediately with barramundi and rice.

Lunch for tomorrow: Sweet potato and bean salad

1. Preheat oven 190°C (375°F). Boil 4 eggs for 6½ minutes, then place in cold water to cool then refrigerate.
2. Cut the sweet potatoes into small chunks and drizzle a tablespoon of exra virgin olive oil.
3. Place into a hot oven for 30–40 minutes. Once cooked and cooled, refrigerate for tommorrow's lunch.

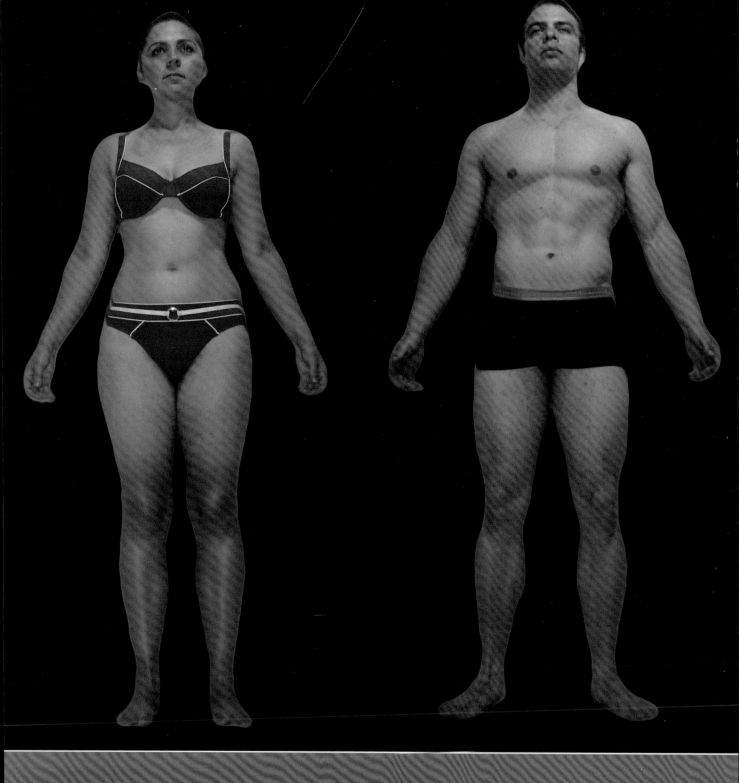

enjoy your food
week 8

Week 8 Overview

DAY	BREAKFAST	LUNCH	DINNER
1	Fresh fruit and seeds	Sweet potato and bean salad	Mackerel pine nut salad
2	Fruit porridge	Tuna and olive salad	Broccoli and chicken stir fry
3	Muesli with fresh fruit	Vegetable soup	Teriyaki burgers
4	Fruit smoothie	Beef salad pitta	Chilli prawns with almonds
5	Fresh fruit and seeds	Mackerel and potato salad	Mustard chicken
6	Omelette	Smoked salmon pitta	Garlic salmon with baked vegetables
7	Wheat biscuits/Shredded Wheat or muesli with a piece of fruit	Tuna salad	Lamb casserole

Snack list

- **Fruits:**

  Melon, mango or coconut – 1 to share

  Peach, plum, or kiwi – 1

  Pineapple – 1 to share (I had 2 slices a week)

  Orange or nectarine – 1

  Berries (blackberries, goji, blueberries, raspberries or strawberries) – 2 portions

  Pear – 1

  Banana – 5

  Apple – 5

- **Dr Karg crackers** – 3
- **Crackers/flat breads** – 1
- **Small bowl of muesli** (if really hungry) – 2
- **Yoghurt/soya yoghurt** (four dessert spoons) – 1
- **Nuts** (cashew, pine or occasionally mixed nuts) – 2 to 3 handfuls
- **Soya nuts** – after all training sessions 3 to 4 handfuls
- **Seeds** (pumpkin or sunflower) – 2 to 3 handfuls
- **Pitta bread/wrap with salad and protein filling** – 1

I would roughly snack four to five times a day at random intervals. On average however, I snacked at 10.00am, 12.00pm, 2.30pm and 4.00pm. You can use this as a guide, but you do not need to snack five times a day – just when you need to.

Shopping List
Week 8

Carbohydrates:

80g almonds
1 bag of brown rice
1 bag of couscous
400g kidney beans
240g of Jordans muesli
1 bag of pine nuts
125g new potatoes
400g pinto beans
560g porridge oats
12 potatoes
1 bag of sunflower seeds
1 bag of pumpkin seeds
8 sweet potatoes
8 wholemeal/brown pitta breads
Wheat biscuits/Shredded wheat

Dairy and non-dairy alternatives:

20 eggs
20g feta/goat's cheese
50g soft goat's/low fat
  cream cheese
880ml skimmed/Alpro soya/rice
  /oat milk
1.7kg Alpro soya yoghurt

Fish:

8 anchovy fillets
4 cooked mackerel
225g fresh mackerel
800g cooked prawns
4 salmon fillets
1 pack smoked salmon (for 4)
1.15kg tuna steaks
4 tinned tuna cans

Meat:

1lb lean minced beef
400g roast beef
8 chicken breasts
400g lean ham
800g leg of lamb

Fruit:

4 apples
1 apricot
8 bananas
1 punnet of blackberries
1 punnet of blueberries
3 lemons
2 limes
2 mangos
1 melon
2 oranges
1 peach
1 large pineapple
1 punnet of raspberries

Vegetables:

2 avocados
600g baby spinach
25g black olives
75g broccoli
250g cherry tomatoes
3 carrots
3 celery sticks
2 courgettes
½ cucumber
175g french beans
2 leeks
3 lettuces
8 large mushrooms
50g mange tout
5 onions
2 parsnips
115g plum tomatoes
3 red onions
4 red peppers
23 tomatoes
100g rocket salad
1 shallot
10 spring onions

Herbs:

Basil
2 bay leaves
Black pepper
Chives
Coriander
Cumin
Fresh ginger
1 garlic clove
Parsley
2 red chillies
Rosemary

Other:

Balsamic vinegar
Chicken stock
Chinese white rice vinegar
Cold pressed extra virgin olive oil
Corn flour
Dijon mustard
Light soy sauce
Peanut oil
60ml red wine
Soy sauce
Sugar
400g tinned tomatoes
Tomato puree
Whole grain mustard

Snacks:

Fruit
Dr Karg crackers
Crackers/flat breads
Small bowl of muesli
Yoghurt/Alpro soya yoghurt
Nuts (cashew, pine or
  occasionally mixed nuts)
Soya nuts
Seeds (pumpkin or sunflower)

Fruit drinks

1 carton Tropicana/Innocent fruit
drink

Your food diary:

Meal   Time   Description

Breakfast:

Snacks:

Lunch:

Snacks:

Dinner:

Snacks:

BREAKFAST

Recipes for Week 8: Day 1

Fresh fruit and seeds

8 tablespoons of soya/plain yoghurt
Sprinkle of sunflower or pumpkin seeds
2 pieces of fruit of your choice per person

1. Mix together the soya/plain yoghurt, seeds and fruit
2. Divide into 4 portions.

LUNCH

Sweet potato and bean salad

4 cooked sweet potatoes
4 eggs
2 avocados, stoned and peeled
400g tinned kidney beans

400g tinned pinto beans
1 small red onion, finely sliced
Coriander, large handful chopped
250g cherry tomatoes, halved

1. Preheat oven 190°C (375°F)
2. Boil 4 eggs for 6½ minutes, then place in cold water to cool slightly.
3. Cut the sweet potatoes into small chunks and drizzle a tablespoon of exra virgin olive oil and place into oven for 30–40 minutes.
4. Slice avocados and place in bowl with beans, sweet potatoes, onions, coriander and tomatoes.
5. Mix in the olive oil, lime juice, chilli and cumin in a small bowl.
6. Once eggs have cooled but are still warm, peel off the shells and cut into quarters.
7. Toss the salad with the dressing, place the eggs on top and serve.

DINNER

Mackerel pine nut salad

4 whole mackerel, scaled and gutted
1 clove of garlic, peeled and sliced
4 tablespoon parsley, chopped
4 spring onions, trimmed and chopped

3 tablespoons pine nuts
1 lemon, zest of
Serve with fresh salad of your choice

1. Preheat the grill to high and cover the grill tray with tin foil.
2. Make 2 incisions in the side of each mackerel and fill with garlic and parsley and place on a tray.
3. Mix the spring onions, pine nuts, lemon zest in a small bowl and use to stuff the cavity of the mackerel.
4. Place fish under the hot grill and cook for 3–4 minutes on each side or until cooked.
5. Remove the mackerel from the grill and allow to cool for a few minutes.
6. Serve fish on top of the fresh salad.

NOTES

Recipes for Week 8: Day 2

Your food diary:

Meal Time Description

Breakfast:

Snacks:

Lunch:

Snacks:

Dinner:

Snacks:

Fruit porridge

240g porridge oats (60g per person)
2–3 apples, chopped
120ml water or milk (soya/rice/oat or skimmed milk) -
  enough to cover the oats and apples

1. Slowly bring to the boil the water and/or milk in a sauce pan.
2. Add the oats and chopped apples.
3. Cook for 10 minutes, stirring continuously until thickened. If the mixture becomes too thick, add more water or milk. Serve immediately.

Tuna and olive salad

175g french beans, topped and tailed
350g fresh tuna steaks
115g baby plum tomatoes, halved
8 anchovy fillets, drained on kitchen paper
25g stoned black olives in brine, drained
Fresh basil, leaves to garnish

For the dressing:
1 tablespoon olive oil
1 garlic clove, crushed
1 tablespoon lemon juice
1 tablespoon basil leaves, shredded

1. Cook the french beans in a small saucepan of boiling water for 5 minutes, or until slightly tender, drain well and keep warm.
2. Season the tuna steaks with black pepper and place tuna on grill rack and cook for 4–5 minutes on each side, or until cooked through.
3. Drain the tuna on kitchen paper and using a knife and fork, flake the tuna into bite size pieces.
4. Mix the tuna, french beans, tomatoes, anchovies and olives into a bowl and keep warm.
5. Mix all the dressing ingredients together. Pour dressing over tuna salad. Garnish with basil and serve.

Broccoli and chicken stir fry

800g skinless chicken breasts, diced
1 head broccoli, broken into florets
1 tablespoon ginger, freshly grated
1 clove garlic, crushed
1 onion, quartered
1 red pepper, deseeded and sliced
2 tablespoons water

2 teaspoons chinese rice wine
1 tablespoon soy sauce
2 teaspoons corn flour
1 teaspoon sesame oil
1 tablespoon peanut oil
Serve with brown rice

1. Bring a small saucepan of water to boil and blanch the broccoli for 2 minutes. Drain, and allow to cool .
2. In a cup, mix together the water, chinese rice wine, soy sauce and corn flour and set aside.
3. Heat a wok or large frying pan over medium heat.
4. Add sesame oil, peanut oil and once smoking, add the ginger and garlic and cook for a few seconds, stirring continuously.
5. Add the chicken and stir fry for 6–8 minutes, or until cooked. Remove from wok and set aside.
6. Boil the rice. Add the onion and red pepper to frying pan and stir-fry for 5 minutes, or until vegetables begin to soften.
7. Next add the broccoli and corn flour and stir until sauce has thickened.
8. Return chicken to the frying pan and heat through. Serve the chicken stir-fry with brown rice.

Lunch for tomorrow: Vegetable soup

1. Bring stock to boil in a large saucepan.
2. Add the carrot, celery, onion, parsley and tomatoes and simmer for 30 minutes.
3. Stir through basil and rosemary and season with black pepper.
4. Allow to cool and refrigerate overnight.

Recipes for Week 8: Day 3

Muesli with fresh fruit

240g muesli (60g per person)
Serving of milk (soya/rice/oat or skimmed milk)
Fruit of your choice, cut into chunks (1 piece of fruit per person)

1. Place muesli in a bowl, add milk.
2. Serve with fruit.

Your food diary:

Meal   Time   Description

Breakfast:

Snacks:

Lunch:

Snacks:

Dinner:

Snacks:

Vegetable soup

1 litre vegetable stock
2 carrots, sliced
2 celery sticks, chopped
1 onion, chopped

1 tablespoon fresh parsley, chopped
400g tin tomatoes
1 tablespoon basil, chopped
1 tablespoon rosemary, finely chopped

1. Bring stock to boil in a large saucepan.
2. Add the carrots, celery, onion, parsley and tomatoes and simmer gently for 30 minutes.
3. Stir through basil and rosemary and season with black pepper.

Teriyaki burgers

1lb (90%) lean ground beef minced
2 tablespoons light soy sauce
1 tablespoon fresh ginger, peeled and grated
1 garlic clove, minced
¼ cup onions, chopped
Pinch of pepper

4 baking potatoes, sliced into wedges
Lettuce leaves
1 small red onion, sliced
3 tomatoes, sliced
20g goat's or mature cheese 5g per person

1. Preheat oven to 190°C (373 F).
2. Boil the potato wedges until partially tender.
3. Place wedges on a baking tray and drizzle over extra virgin olive oil.
4. Cook in the oven until crisp and golden.
5. Combine all the ingredients for the burgers in a bowl.
6. Form into 4 to 8 patties and grill for 5 minutes one side then turn over.
7. Place the feta/goat's cheese or mature goat's cheese on the uncooked side and cook for a further 5 minutes or until cheese has melted.
8. Serve burgers with wedges and salad.

Recipes for Week 8: Day 4

BREAKFAST

Fruit smoothie

2 large mangos, peeled and chopped

4 bananas, chopped

2 handfuls of raspberries

Blend mangos, bananas and raspberries and serve.

LUNCH

Beef salad pitta

4 wholemeal pitta breads, hot or cold

400g cold roast beef, finely sliced

Generous amounts of green salad
 (cos lettuce, rocket, baby spinach, etc)

4 large tomatoes, sliced

1 red pepper, sliced

½ small red onion, finely sliced

2 tablespoons basil, chopped

For the dressing:

2 tablespoons olive oil

1 tablespoon balsamic vinegar

1 clove garlic, crushed

1 teaspoon dijon mustard

Season with black pepper

1. In a small bowl, mix all the dressing ingredients.
2. Put the remaining ingredients in a large salad bowl and toss.
3. Slice open the pitta bread and fill with beef and salad.
4. Pour the dressing over the top and serve.

DINNER

Chilli prawns with almonds

1 red chilli, finely chopped

1 tablespoon olive oil

1 onion, chopped

2 garlic cloves, roughly chopped

8 tomatoes, roughly chopped

1 teaspoon ground cumin

100ml chicken stock

80g ground almonds

150ml soya/plain yoghurt

800g cooked peeled prawns

1 lime

Serve with brown rice and vegetables

1. Heat the olive oil in a frying pan over medium heat.
2. Add the garlic, chilli and onion and cook until soft.
3. Next add the tomatoes and ground cumin and cook for 10 minutes, stirring occasionally.
4. Add the stock to the mixture and blend in a food processor until smooth.
5. Pour the mixture into a large saucepan adding the ground almonds and stir over a low heat for 2 minutes.
6. Gently stir in the yoghurt.
7. Squeeze the juice from the lime and stir into sauce.
8. Increase the heat and simmer.
9. Add the prawns and heat for 2–3 minutes until warmed through.
10. Serve with brown rice and vegetables.

PREPARE

Lunch for tomorrow: Mackerel and potato salad

1. Boil or steam the new potatoes in a saucepan.
2. Refrigerate overnight and serve for tomorrow's lunch.

Recipes for Week 8: Day 5

Fresh fruit and seeds

8 tablespoons of soya/plain yoghurt
Sprinkle of sunflower or pumpkin seeds
2 pieces of fruit of your choice per person

1. Mix together the yoghurt, seeds and fruit
2. Divide into 4 portions.

Mackerel and potato salad

125g new potatoes, scrubbed and diced
225g fresh mackerel fillets, remove skin
1.2 litres water
1 eating apple, cored and diced
1 shallot, thinly sliced
3 tablespoons white wine vinegar
¼ teaspoon dijon mustard

2 tablespoons low fat soya/plain yoghurt
¼ cucumber, thinly sliced
1 bay leaf
1 slice of lemon
1 tablespoon fresh chives, chopped
1 ½ teaspoons brown sugar
1 teaspoon olive oil

1. Steam the potatoes over a saucepan of simmering water for 10 minutes.
2. Bring water to the boil in another saucepan, then reduce the heat to simmer adding the mackerel pieces, bay leaf and lemon.
3. Poach for 3 minutes or until flesh is opaque. Remove fish from saucepan and transfer to serving dish.
4. Drain the potatoes and transfer to a large bowl.
5. Mix the apple and shallot and then spoon the mixture over the mackerel.
6. Next mix the vinegar, olive oil, sugar and mustard together in bowl and whisk thoroughly.
7. Pour dressing over potato mixture.
8. Serve with salad, soya/plain yoghurt dressing, put cucumber on the top and sprinkle with fresh chives.

Mustard chicken

1 tablespoon olive oil
4 chicken breasts, remove any fat
2 large oranges, peel and cut into segments,
   reserve the juice
2 teaspoons cornflour

150ml soya/plain yoghurt
1 teaspoon wholegrain mustard
Parsley to garnish
Serve with couscous, salad or vegetables
 of your choice

1. Heat the olive oil in a large frying pan and add the chicken breasts.
2. Cook over medium to high heat for 5 minutes each side, or until tender and juices run clear.
3. Season with black pepper then remove chicken from frying pan and cover with foil and keep warm.
4. Pour the orange juice into a bowl and stir in the corn flour to make a smooth paste.
5. Stir in soya/plain soya/plain yoghurt and mustard then pour into the frying pan. Bring to boil over a low heat while stirring.
6. Add the orange segments to the frying pan and season to taste with pepper.
7. Stir in the juices from the chicken. Spoon the sauce on to 4 large plates and top with chicken.
8. Serve with salad or vegetables and couscous and garnish with parsley.

Lunch for tomorrow: Yellow split pea soup

Pre-soak 225g of yellow split peas overnight in cold water.

Recipes for Week 8: Day 6

BREAKFAST

Omelette

8 eggs (2 eggs per person)
4 tablespoons water, of cold
8 teaspoons olive oil
400g lean ham
1 courgette, finely sliced
4 spring onions, finely chopped
Parsley to garnish

1. Cook omelette for one person at a time. Beat the eggs with water in a bowl.
2. Heat the olive oil in a non stick pan over a high heat.
3. Pour in eggs and cook for 2 minutes or until mixture just begins to set.
4. Place ham and courgette on top of the egg mixture and cook until omelette has set.
5. Sprinkle on parsley and spring onions.
6. Fold omelette in half and serve. Repeat process.

LUNCH

Smoked salmon pitta

4 wholemeal pitta breads (hot or cold)
Smoked salmon
Soft goat's/low fat soft cheese (small serving per person)
2 spring onions, finely sliced

200g baby spinach
4 large tomatoes, sliced into quarters
1 red pepper, finely sliced

1. Slice open pitta bread and spread the goat's cheese thinly across one side.
2. Add the smoke salmon and sprinkle over the spring onions.
3. Serve with spinach, tomatoes and red pepper.

DINNER

Garlic salmon with baked vegetables

2 leeks, washed, trimmed and sliced
500g baby spinach leaves
4 x 100g salmon fillets
1 tablespoon olive oil
2 garlic cloves, peeled and finely chopped

1 tablespoon fresh ginger, grated
1 lemon, juice of
Coriander to garnish
Serve with couscous

1. Preheat the oven to 200°C (400°F).
2. Gently boil or steam the leeks for 5 minutes.
3. Arrange the spinach leaves in a baking tray, then add the leeks and place salmon on top.
4. Mix together the olive oil, garlic and ginger in a small bowl and brush mixture over the salmon using pastry brush.
5. Pour over the lemon juice, place in the oven and cook for 10 minutes.
6. Boil and cook couscous.
7. Remove from oven and leave to cool for a few minutes.
8. Serve with couscous and garnish with fresh coriander.

NOTES

Recipes for Week 8: Day 7

Wheat biscuits, Shredded Wheat or muesli with fruit

560ml milk (soya/rice/oat or skimmed milk)
2–3 wheat biscuits/Shredded Wheat or 240g of muesli, (60g per person)
1 piece of fruit of your choice

Place oats or cereal in a bowl add milk and serve with fruit.

Tuna salad

4 cooked sweet potatoes
4 small tinned tuna
1 tablespoon balsamic vinegar
1 tablespoon olive oil

Side salad:
100g of rocket leaves
4 tomatoes, roughly chopped
¼ cucumber, roughly chopped
50g mange-tout
1 red pepper, sliced

1. Preheat oven 190°C (375°F).
2. Cut the sweet potatoes into small chunks and drizzle a tablespoon of exra virgin olive oil and place into oven for 30–40 minutes.
3. Once cooked, allow to cool and place into the fridge for tommorrow's lunch.
4. Place rocket leaves, mange-tout, tomatoes, cucumber and red pepper in a salad bowl and gently mix with balsamic vinegar and olive.
5. Serve with the tuna and sweet potatoes.

Lamb casserole

800g lean lamb leg, diced
2 tablespoons olive oil
1 onion, finely chopped
1 carrot, finely chopped
1 celery stick, finely chopped
2 cloves garlic, crushed
60ml red wine
2 tablespoons tomato puree

450ml chicken stock
1 bay leaf
2 sprigs rosemary
Water
2 parsnips, peeled and chopped
2 tablespoons parsley
Serve with potatoes

1. Preheat oven to 180°C (350°F).
2. Heat a large saucepan over a high heat.
3. Coat lamb with olive oil and cook in small batches for 5 minutes or until browned.
4. Remove from pan and set aside.
5. Add the onion, carrot, celery to the pan and cook for 5 minutes, or until soft
6. Next return lamb to pan adding the garlic, red wine and tomato puree and cook for a further 5 minutes.
7. Add the chicken stock, bay leaf, rosemary and enough water to ensure lamb is covered.
8. Cover with lid and bake in the oven for 1 hour.
9. Add the parsnips and cook for a further 40 minutes.
10. Serve with potatoes and sprinkle with parsley.

enjoy your food
week 9

Week 9 Overview

DAY	BREAKFAST	LUNCH	DINNER
1	Fresh fruit and seeds	Beetroot salad	Coconut monkfish
2	Fruit smoothie	Yellow split pea soup	Chicken with coriander
3	Muesli with fresh fruit	Egg salad	Cajun fish
4	Wheat biscuits/Shredded Wheat or muesli with a piece of fruit	Salmon salad	Thai beef salad
5	Fruit porridge	Tuna salad	Spicy tomato chicken
6	Omelette	Butternut squash and coriander soup	Salmon with asparagus
7	Fruit salad	Chicken salad pitta	Ginger turkey curry

Snack list

- **Fruits:**

    Melon, mango or coconut – 1 to share

    Peach, plum, or kiwi – 1

    Pineapple – 1 to share (I had 2 slices a week)

    Orange or nectarine – 1

    Berries (blackberries, goji, blueberries, raspberries or strawberries) – 2 portions

    Pear – 1

    Banana – 5

    Apple – 5
- **Dr Karg crackers** – 3
- **Crackers/flat breads** – 1
- **Small bowl of muesli** (if really hungry) – 2
- **Yoghurt/soya yoghurt** (four dessert spoons) – 1
- **Nuts** (cashew, pine or occasionally mixed nuts) – 2 to 3 handfuls
- **Soya nuts** – after all training sessions 3 to 4 handfuls
- **Seeds** (pumpkin or sunflower) – 2 to 3 handfuls
- **Pitta bread/wrap with salad and protein filling** – 1

I would roughly snack four to five times a day at random intervals. On average however, I snacked at 10.00am, 12.00pm, 2.30pm and 4.00pm. You can use this as a guide, but you do not need to snack five times a day – just when you need to.

Shopping List
Week 9

Carbohydrates:

1 bag of brown rice
1 bag of couscous
260g of Jordans muesli
560g porridge oats
12 potatoes
1 bag of sunflower seeds
1 bag of pumpkin seeds
5 sweet potatoes
4 wholemeal/brown pitta breads
225g yellow split peas
1 bag of wild rice
Wheat biscuits/Shredded wheat

Dairy and non-dairy alternatives:

12 eggs
2105ml skimmed/Alpro soya/rice /oat milk
2kg Alpro soya yoghurt

Fish:

6 anchovy fillets
4 monkfish tails
225g raw peeled prawns
4 poached salmon fillets
200g x 4 salmon steaks
4 tins tuna
450g white fish of your choice

Meat:

800g rump beef steak
8 chicken breasts
400g lean ham
400g turkey breast

Fruit:

8 apples
2 apricots
6 bananas
1 punnet of blackberries
1 punnet of blueberries
4 lemons
2 limes
1 melon
2 oranges
2 peaches
1 large pineapple
1 punnet of raspberries

Vegetables:

16 asparagus spears
1 avocado
1 baby gem lettuce
350g baby spinach
150g bean sprouts
4 cooked beetroots
1.4kg butternut squash
650g cherry tomatoes
5 carrots
2 celery sticks
1 courgette
1½ cucumbers
3 lettuce
50g mange tout
4 onions
115g plum tomatoes
3 red onions
4 red peppers
5 red tomatoes
100g rocket salad
5 shallots
11 spring onions
5 yellow peppers

Fruit drinks

1 carton Tropicana/Innocent fruit drink

Herbs:

Chilli powder
Chives
Coriander
Ground coriander
Cumin
Curry powder
Fresh ginger
1 garlic clove
1 green chilli
Mint
Nutmeg
Paprika
Parsley
1 red chilli
Rosemary
Turmeric

Other:

Balsamic vinegar
Chicken stock
Cider vinegar
150ml coconut milk
Cold pressed extra virgin olive oil
Corn flour
Dijon mustard
Fish sauce
Honey
115ml lemon juice
Soy sauce
Tomato puree
Vegetable stock
Worchester sauce

Snacks:

Fruit
Dr Karg crackers
Crackers/flat breads
Small bowl of muesli
Yoghurt/Alpro soya yoghurt
Nuts (cashew, pine or occasionally mixed nuts)
Soya nuts
Seeds (pumpkin or sunflower)

Recipes for Week 9: Day 1

Fresh fruit and seeds

8 tablespoons of soya/plain yoghurt
Sprinkle of sunflower or pumpkin seeds
2 pieces of fruit of your choice per person

1. Mix together the soya/plain yoghurt, seeds and fruit
2. Divide into 4 portions.

Your food diary:

Meal   Time   Description

Breakfast:

Snacks:

Lunch:

Snacks:

Dinner:

Snacks:

Beetroot salad

100g brown rice
100g wild rice
4 shallots, peeled and halved
2 teaspoons olive oil

4 cooked beetroot, finely diced
1 lemon, juice of
2 tablespoons fresh mint, chopped
2 tablespoons fresh chives, chopped

1. Preheat oven to 200°C (400°F).
2. Place brown and wild rice in medium sauce pan of water. Bring to boil and simmer for 20 – 30 minutes.
3. Place the shallots on a baking tray, drizzle with olive oil and roast for 8-10 minutes.
4. Drain the rice and allow to cool.
5. Gently mix together the beetroot, lemon juice and mint.
6. Stir in shallots and chives and serve.

Coconut monkfish

450g/1lb monkfish tails, cut into chunks
225g/8oz raw peeled prawns
1 red pepper, chunks to go onto skewers
1 yellow pepper, chunks to go onto skewers
1 red onion, chunks to go onto skewers

For the marinade:
1 teaspoon olive oil
½ small onion, finely grated
1 teaspoon fresh ginger, grated
150ml/5fl oz canned coconut milk
2 tablespoons fresh coriander, chopped
Serve with salad and couscous

1. To make the marinade: heat the olive oil in a large saucepan and fry the onion and ginger for 5 minutes, or until just soft not brown.
2. Add the coconut milk to the saucepan and bring to the boil.
3. Boil rapidly for 5 minutes then remove from heat and allow to cool completely.
4. Once cold, stir in the coriander into the coconut milk and pour into a shallow dish.
5. Gently stir in monkfish and prawns into the coconut mixture and cover.
6. Leave to marinate in the fridge for 1–4 hours.
7. Preheat grill to medium.
8. Thread the fish and prawns on to skewers with the red onion, red and yellow peppers.
9. Cook the skewers under the preheated grill for 10–15 minutes, turning frequently.
10. Garnish with toasted desiccated coconut and serve on a bed of salad and couscous.

Lunch for tomorrow: Yellow split pea soup

Pre-soak 225g of yellow split peas overnight in cold water.

BREAKFAST

LUNCH

DINNER

PREPARE

Recipes for Week 9: Day 2

Fruit smoothie

4 tablespoons nut and seed muesli
1200ml milk (soya/rice/oat or skimmed milk)
2 bananas
2 apricots
2 peaches

1. Mix the muesli and milk in a blender until nearly smooth.
2. Add the bananas, peaches and apricots and blend until completely smooth.
3. If the smoothie is too thick, add more water.

Yellow split pea soup

225g yellow split peas
  (Pre-soak for 12 hours overnight in cold water)
1.5 litres of vegetable stock
1 onion, peeled and sliced

1 sweet potato, peeled and chopped
3 carrots, trimmed, peeled and sliced
Fresh mint
Fresh baby spinach leaves, 4 handfuls

1. Drain water from the split peas.
2. Bring the vegetable stock to boil in a large saucepan and add split peas.
3. Simmer for 25 minutes removing any scum on the surface.
4. Add all other vegetables to the saucepan and simmer for a further 15–20 minutes or until vegetables are tender. Remove from heat and allow to cool.
5. Blend soup with food processor or blender.
6. Reheat soup and add the spinach. Serve with a mint garnish.

Chicken with coriander

1 tablespoon olive oil
4 skinless, boneless chicken breasts
  115g/4oz each, trim off the fat
1 teaspoon cornflour
1 tablespoon water
100ml soya/plain yoghurt
175ml/6fl oz chicken stock

2 tablespoons lime juice
2 garlic cloves, finely chopped
1 tomato, peeled, deseeded and chopped
1 shallot, finely chopped
Fresh coriander, 1 bunch of chopped
Serve with salad of your choice

1. Heat the olive oil in a large frying pan then add the chicken and cook over medium heat for 5 minutes each side or until cooked.
2. Remove chicken from frying pan and keep warm.
3. Mix the corn flour and water until smooth. Stir in the soya/plain soya/plain yoghurt.
4. Pour the chicken stock and lime juice into frying pan and add the garlic and shallot.
5. Reduce the heat and simmer for 1 minute then add the tomato and stir in with mixture.
6. Cook and stir constantly for 1–2 minutes. Do not let the mixture boil.
7. Stir in the fresh coriander.
8. Serve the chicken with the salad, pour sauce over and garnish with fresh coriander.

Lunch for tomorrow: Egg salad

1. Boil the 4 eggs for 6½ minutes
2. Place in cold water and allow to cool.
3. Refrigerate overnight.

Recipes for Week 9: Day 3

BREAKFAST

Muesli with fresh fruit

240g muesli (60g per person)
Serving of milk (soya/rice/oat or skimmed milk)
Fruit of your choice, cut into chunks (1 piece of fruit per person)

1. Place muesli in a bowl, add milk.
2. Serve with fruit.

LUNCH

Egg salad

4 baby gem lettuce
200g baby spinach
150g cherry tomatoes, halved
4 shelled hard boiled eggs, cut into quarters
½ cucumber, sliced
1 yellow pepper, deseeded and sliced

For the dressing:
1 tablespoon dijon mustard
1 tablespoon olive oil
2 teaspoons cider vinegar
1 teaspoon water

1. Arrange the lettuce, spinach, tomatoes, yellow pepper, and cucumber on plates.
2. Mix the mustard and water add mix in the olive oil and vinegar into a small bowl.
3. Put the eggs on top of the salad, drizzle with the dressing and serve.

DINNER

Cajun fish

225ml soya/skimmed milk
800g white fish fillets
(snapper, whiting, flathead etc)
2 tablespoons olive oil
400g soya/plain yoghurt
½ cucumber, finely diced

Spices:
1 tablespoon paprika
2 teaspoons ground cumin
1 teaspoon chilli powder
Serve with salad or vegetables of your choice

1. Preheat oven to 200°C (400°F).
2. Line a baking tray with baking paper.
3. Pour the milk in a small bowl while in a separate bowl, mix the ground spices.
4. Dip the fish fillets into the milk then roll in the mixed spices.
5. Heat the olive oil in a large frying pan over a high heat and fry the fish quickly in batches, for 2 minutes each side, or until golden. Be careful not overcrowd the pan, as the fish will stew.
6. Place the fish fillets on the baking tray and bake for 5 minutes.
7. Mix soya/plain yoghurt and cucumber to make the dressing.
8. Serve the fish with salad and pour over soya/plain yoghurt dressing.

NOTES

Your food diary:
Meal   Time   Description
Breakfast:

Snacks:

Lunch:

Snacks:

Dinner:

Snacks:

BREAKFAST

LUNCH

DINNER

PREPARE

Recipes for Week 9: Day 4

Wheat biscuits, Shredded Wheat or muesli with fruit

560ml milk (soya/rice/oat or skimmed milk)
2-3 wheat biscuits/Shredded Wheat or 240g of Muesli, (60g per person)
1 piece of fruit of your choice

Place oats or cereal in a bowl add milk and serve with fruit.

Salmon salad

200g mixed salad leaves
250g cherry tomatoes, halved
Coriander, a handful roughly chopped
2–3 spring onions, finely sliced
¼ cucumber, roughly chopped
4 cooked poach salmon fillets, cut into bite size pieces
2 yellow peppers, sliced

For the dressing:
500g soya/plain yoghurt
2 tablespoons coriander, chopped
1 garlic clove, finely chopped
4 teaspoons lemon juice
1 teaspoon ground cumin

1. Place all ingredients in a bowl and mix well, season with black pepper.
2. Cover and refrigerate for 5–10 minutes before using. If the sauce is too thick, add some water to thin it out.
3. Place salad leaves, cherry tomatoes, coriander, spring onions, salmon, cucumber and yellow peppers in a salad bowl and toss. Serve the salad and salmon fillets and pour dressing over the dressing.

Thai beef salad

800g lean rump steak
1 tablespoon olive oil
For the salad:
100g spinach leaves
1 red pepper, deseeded and finely sliced
150g bean sprouts
4 spring onions, finely sliced
125g fresh coriander
2 tablespoons mint, chopped

For the dressing:
2 tablespoons lime juice
1 tablespoon fish sauce
1 tablespoon soy sauce
1 clove garlic, crushed
1 red chilli, deseeded and chopped

1. Preheat the grill to high.
2. Brush the steak with olive oil and cook for 3–4 minutes each side, or cook to your liking.
3. Remove from the heat and cover steak with tin foil and leave to rest for 5 minutes.
4. Meanwhile, mix all the dressing ingredients in a small bowl.
5. Slice the steak across the grain into thin strips. Place the beef and remaining ingredients in a large bowl.
6. Pour dressing over the salad gently toss and serve.

Lunch for tomorrow: Tuna salad

Preheat oven 190°C (375°F).
1. Cut the sweet potatoes into small chunks and put in an ovenproof dish.
2. Drizzle over a tablespoon of exra virgin olive oil. Place into oven for 30–40 minutes.
3. Once cooked place and cooled place into the fridge for tommorrow's lunch .

Recipes for Week 9: Day 5

Fruit porridge

240g of porridge oats (60g per person)

2–3 apples, chopped

120ml of water or milk (soya/rice/oat or skimmed milk) – enough to cover the oats and apples

1. Slowly bring to the boil the water and/or milk in a sauce pan.
2. Add the oats and chopped apples.
3. Cook for 10 minutes, stirring continuously until thickened. If the mixture becomes too thick, add more water or milk.
4. Serve immediately.

Tuna salad

4 cooked sweet potatoes

4 small tins tuna

1 tablespoon balsamic vinegar

1 tablespoon olive oil

Side salad:

100g of rocket leaves

4 tomatoes, roughly chopped

¼ cucumber, roughly chopped

50g mange-tout

1 red pepper, sliced

1. Preheat oven 190°C (375°F).
2. Cut the sweet potatoes into small chunks and drizzle a tablespoon of exra virgin olive oil and place into oven for 30–40 minutes.
3. Once cooked, allow to cool and place into the fridge for tommorrow's lunch.
4. Place rocket leaves, mange-tout, tomatoes, cucumber and red pepper in a salad bowl and gently mix with balsamic vinegar and olive oil.
5. Serve with the tuna and sweet potatoes.

Spicy tomato chicken

500g boneless chicken breasts, diced

3 tablespoons tomato puree

2 tablespoons clear honey

2 tablespoons Worcestershire sauce

1 tablespoon rosemary, chopped

250g cherry tomatoes

Serve with salad

8 wooden skewers

1. Mix together the tomato puree, honey, Worcestershire sauce and rosemary in a bowl.
2. Add the diced chicken and coat evenly.
3. Preheat the grill to medium.
4. Thread the chicken and the cherry tomatoes on the wooden skewers and place them on grill rack.
5. Spoon the honey mixture over the chicken skewers and grill for 8–10 minutes, turning occasionally until chicken is cooked through.
6. Serve the spicy tomato chicken with a salad.

BREAKFAST

LUNCH

DINNER

Recipes for Week 9: Day 6

Omelette

8 eggs (2 eggs per person)
4 tablespoons of cold water
8 teaspoons of extra virgin olive oil cold pressed
400g lean ham
1 courgette, finely sliced
4 spring onions, finely chopped

1. Cook one omelette at a time, beat the eggs with some water in a bowl.
2. Heat the extra virgin olive oil in a non stick pan over a high heat and pour in the eggs. Cook for 2 minutes or until the mixture just begins to set.
3. Place ham and courgette on top of the egg mixture and cook until omelette has set.
4. Sprinkle on the spring onions, fold omelette in half and serve.

Butternut squash and coriander soup

900ml chicken stock
1kg butternut squash, peeled and roughly chopped
1 onion, roughly chopped
2 carrots, roughly chopped
2 celery sticks, roughly chopped

1 garlic clove, finely chopped
1 teaspoon paprika
½ teaspoon turmeric
½ teaspoon ground coriander
½ teaspoon ground nutmeg

1. In a large saucepan, bring chicken stock to boil.
2. Add vegetables and spices and bring back to boil.
3. Reduce heat and simmer for 20 minutes, or until vegetables are soft.
4. Allow to cool and then blend.
5. Reheat soup and serve.

Salmon with asparagus

400g butternut squash,
  peeled and cut into thick slices
1 tablespoon olive oil
4 x 200g salmon fillets
16 asparagus spears

For the relish:
Fresh parsley, 1 bunch
6 anchovy fillets
2 lemons, grated zest
115ml lemon juice
60ml olive oil

1. To make relish: place all ingredients except olive oil in a food processor and lightly process.
2. Then add olive oil to form a thick paste.
3. Preheat oven to 180°C (350°F).
4. Place the butternut squash in a bowl and coat with half the amount of olive oil.
5. Transfer to baking dish and cook for 20 minutes or until soft.
6. Meanwhile turn grill to high and lightly brush the salmon with the remaining olive oil.
7. Place salmon in grill and cook for 4 minutes each side.
8. Remove from heat cover and set aside.
9. Bring a saucepan of water to boil, add the asparagus and blanch for 2 minutes, then drain.
10. Arrange the salmon, asparagus and pumpkin slices on a serving plate and enjoy!

Recipes for Week 9: Day 7

Your food diary:

Meal   Time   Description

Breakfast:

Snacks:

Lunch:

Snacks:

Dinner:

Snacks:

Fruit salad

8 tablespoons soya yoghurt (2 tablespoons per person)

80g oats

60g sunflower seeds or pumpkin seeds

4-5 pieces of fruit (preferably ones in season)

1. Dice fruit into chunks and divide into 4 portions.
2. Add 2 tablespoons of soya yoghurt in each portion and sprinkle with oats and seeds.

Chicken salad pitta

4 wholemeal pitta breads (served hot or cold)

4 chicken breasts, cut into small pieces

Generous amount of salad leaves

1 avocado, sliced

1 red pepper, sliced

1 yellow pepper, sliced

2 spring onions, finely chopped

½ tablespoon olive oil

1. Heat olive oil in a frying pan over a medium heat.
2. Cook the chicken for 8–12 minutes, or until cooked.
3. Remove from heat and set aside to rest for 5 minutes.
4. Meanwhile, prepare the salad.
5. Slice open the pitta bread and fill with the chicken and salad.
6. Serve immediately.

Ginger turkey curry

400g turkey fillet

½ tablespoon olive oil

1 onion, sliced

1 green chilli, finely sliced

12cm ginger, peeled and sliced

1 clove garlic, peeled and chopped

3 teaspoons curry powder

300ml chicken or vegetable stock

300g brown or wild rice

Coriander, big bunch

5 tablespoons soya/plain yoghurt

Serve with rice

1. Heat the olive oil and add the onion, ginger, chilli and garlic. Cook on medium heat for 10 minutes. Do not allow to burn.
2. Slice the turkey into small pieces and add to the pan with curry powder and cook for 5 minutes.
3. Add the stock, bring to the boil and simmer for 15 minutes.
4. Cook the rice on medium heat for 15–20 minutes or until cooked.
5. Stir in the yoghurt and chopped coriander through the turkey curry and serve.

Lunch for tomorrow: Butternut squash and coriander soup

1. In a large saucepan, bring chicken stock to boil.
2. Add the vegetables and spices and bring back to boil.
3. Reduce heat and simmer for 20 minutes or until vegetables are soft.
4. Allow to cool and blend in a food processor.
5. Refrigerate overnight.

enjoy your food
week 10

Week 10 Overview

DAY	BREAKFAST	LUNCH	DINNER
1	Fruit porridge	Butternut squash and coriander soup	Sword fish with courgette salad
2	Fruit salad	Beetroot salad	Baked lamb and vegetables
3	Muesli with fresh fruit	Beef salad pitta	Poached chicken
4	Wheat biscuits/Shredded Wheat or muesli with a piece of fruit	Chicken wrap	Marlin steaks
5	Fresh fruit and seeds	Tuna and olive salad	Baked mediterranean vegetables with ricotta and turkey
6	Omelette	Vegetable soup	Monkfish delight
7	Fruit smoothie	Tuna salad	Garlic lamb

Snack list

- **Fruits:**

  Melon, mango or coconut – 1 to share

  Peach, plum, or kiwi – 1

  Pineapple – 1 to share (I had 2 slices a week)

  Orange or nectarine – 1

  Berries (blackberries, goji, blueberries, raspberries or strawberries) – 2 portions

  Pear – 1

  Banana – 5

  Apple – 5

- **Dr Karg crackers** – 3
- **Crackers/flat breads** – 1
- **Small bowl of muesli** (if really hungry) – 2
- **Yoghurt/soya yoghurt** (four dessert spoons) – 1
- **Nuts** (cashew, pine or occasionally mixed nuts) – 2 to 3 handfuls
- **Soya nuts** – after all training sessions 3 to 4 handfuls
- **Seeds** (pumpkin or sunflower) – 2 to 3 handfuls
- **Pitta bread/wrap with salad and protein filling** – 1

I would roughly snack four to five times a day at random intervals. On average however, I snacked at 10.00am, 12.00pm, 2.30pm and 4.00pm. You can use this as a guide, but you do not need to snack five times a day – just when you need to.

Shopping List
Week 10

Carbohydrates:

1 bag of brown rice
1 bag of couscous
240g of Jordans muesli
560g porridge oats
4 potatoes
1 bag of sunflower seeds
1 bag of pumpkin seeds
4 sweet potatoes
4 organic tortilla wraps
4 wholemeal/brown pitta breads
1 bag of wild rice
Wheat biscuits/Shredded wheat

Dairy and non-dairy alternatives:

8 eggs
200g ricotta cheese/goat's cheese
680ml skimmed/Alpro soya/rice/ oat milk
1.5kg Alpro soya yoghurt

Fish:

8 anchovy fillets
350g cod or haddock
4 marlin steaks
350g monkfish
16 large raw prawns
4 x 200g swordfish steaks
4 tins tuna

Meat:

400g cooked roast beef
8 chicken breasts
400g lean ham
350g boneless lamb
800g rack of lamb
4 turkey breasts

Fruit:

6 apples
1 apricot
8 bananas
1 punnet of blackberries
4 lemons
2 limes
2 mangos
2 oranges
1 peach
1 large pineapple
1 punnet of raspberries
1 watermelon

Vegetables:

2 aubergines
200g baby carrots
4 cooked beetroots
1kg butternut squash
24 black olives
4 carrots
8 celery sticks
8 courgettes
1 cucumber
75g french beans
200g green beans
1 green pepper
2 lettuce
50g mange tout
6 onions
200g peas
150g plum tomatoes
4 red onions
4 red peppers
14 red tomatoes
100g rocket salad
4 shallots
10 spring onions
2 yellow peppers

Herbs:

Basil
Black pepper
Chilli powder
Chives
Cinnamon sticks
Ground coriander
Cumin
Fresh ginger
1 garlic clove
1 green chilli
Mint
Nutmeg
Oregano
Paprika
Parsley
Rosemary
Tarragon
Thyme sprigs
Turmeric

Other:

175g dried apricots
Balsamic vinegar
Chicken stock
Chinese rice vinegar
Cold pressed extra virgin olive oil
Dijon mustard
Fish stock
Honey
Light soy sauce
Plain flour
60ml red wine
Soy sauce
Sugar
Tabasco sauce
400g tinned tomatoes
Tomato puree
Vegetable stock

Snacks:

Fruit
Dr Karg crackers
Crackers/flat breads
Small bowl of muesli
Yoghurt/Alpro soya yoghurt
Nuts (cashew, pine or occasionally mixed nuts)
Soya nuts
Seeds (pumpkin or sunflower)

Fruit drinks

1 carton Tropicana/Innocent fruit drink

BREAKFAST

Recipes for Week 10: Day 1

Your food diary:

Meal   Time   Description

Breakfast:

Snacks:

Lunch:

Snacks:

Dinner:

Snacks:

Fruit porridge

240g of porridge oats (60g per person)

2–3 apples, chopped

120ml of water or milk (soya/rice/oat or skimmed milk) –
enough to cover the oats and apples

1. Slowly bring to the boil the water and/or milk in a sauce pan.
2. Add the oats and chopped apples.

3. Cook for 10 minutes, stirring continuously until thickened. If the mixture becomes too thick, add more water or milk.
4. Serve immediately.

Butternut squash and coriander soup

900ml chicken stock

1kg butternut squash, peeled and roughly chopped

1 onion, roughly chopped

2 carrots, roughly chopped

2 celery sticks, roughly chopped

1 garlic clove, finely chopped

1 teaspoon paprika

½ teaspoon turmeric

½ teaspoon ground coriander

½ teaspoon ground nutmeg

1. In a large saucepan, bring chicken stock to boil.
2. Add vegetables and spices and bring back to boil.
3. Reduce heat and simmer for 20 minutes, or until vegetables are soft.

4. Allow to cool and then blend.
5. Reheat soup and serve.

Swordfish with courgette salad

4 x 200g swordfish steaks

1 tablespoon olive oil

Lemon wedges

2 tablespoons fresh parsley, chopped

Couscous

For the salad:

2 teaspoons olive oil

2 tablespoons lemon juice

½ red onion, finely sliced

12 olives (optional)

3 small courgettes

1. To make salad, combine the olive oil, lemon juice, onion and olives in a bowl.
2. Steam the courgettes until tender.
3. Transfer to salad mixture and toss to coat.
4. Boil and cook couscous.

5. Heat a non stick frying pan over medium heat and brush swordfish steaks with oil and pan fry for 2 minutes each side.
6. Toss the parsley through courgette salad and spoon onto serving plates.
7. Place swordfish on top of salad and serve with lemon wedges to garnish.

BREAKFAST

LUNCH

DINNER

NOTES

Recipes for Week 10: Day 2

Your food diary:

Meal	Time	Description
Breakfast:		
Snacks:		
Lunch:		
Snacks:		
Dinner:		
Snacks:		

Fruit salad

8 tablespoons soya yoghurt (2 tablespoons per person)

80g oats

60g sunflower seeds or pumpkin seeds

4-5 pieces of fruit (preferably ones in season)

1. Dice fruit into chunks and divide into 4 portions.
2. Add 2 tablespoons of soya yoghurt in each portion and sprinkle with oats and seeds.

Beetroot salad

100g brown rice

100g wild rice

4 shallots, peeled and halved

2 teaspoons olive oil

4 cooked beetroot, finely diced

1 lemon, juice

2 tablespoons mint, chopped

2 tablespoons chives, chopped

1. Preheat oven to 200°C (400°F).
2. Place brown and wild rice in medium sauce pan of water. Bring to boil and simmer for 20–30 minutes.
3. Place the shallots on a baking tray, drizzle with olive oil and roast for 8–10 minutes.
4. Drain the rice and allow to cool.
5. Gently mix together the beetroot, lemon juice and mint.
6. Stir in shallots and chives and serve.

Baked lamb and vegetables

1 tablespoon olive oil

4 thyme sprigs, chopped

1 tablespoon tarragon, chopped

1 tablespoon parsley, chopped

1 clove garlic

1 lemon, zest finely grated

800g rack of lamb (200g per person), remove fat

200g baby carrots

200g green beans

200g peas

1. Preheat oven to 200°C (400°F).
2. In a bowl mix half the oil with herbs, garlic and lemon zest.
3. Heat a large frying pan over a high heat.
4. Coat lamb in remaining oil and sear until golden on both sides.
5. Transfer to a baking dish and rub herb mixture into lamb rack and bake for 25 minutes.
6. Remove from oven, cover loosely with foil and set aside for 10 minutes.
7. Bring a large saucepan of water to boil and cook carrots for 2 minutes, adding the beans and peas and cook for a further 4 minutes.
8. Drain and serve with the lamb.

Recipes for Week 10: Day 3

Muesli with fresh fruit

240g muesli (60g per person)
Serving of milk (soya/rice/oat or skimmed milk)
Fruit of your choice, cut into chunks (1 piece of fruit per person)

1. Place muesli in a bowl, add milk.
2. Serve with fruit.

Beef salad pitta

4 wholemeal pitta breads, hot or cold
400g cold roast beef, finely sliced
Generous amounts of green salad
 (cos lettuce, rocket, baby spinach, etc)
4 large tomatoes, sliced
1 red pepper, sliced
½ small red onion, finely sliced
2 tablespoons basil, chopped

For the dressing:
2 tablespoons olive oil
1 tablespoon balsamic vinegar
1 clove garlic, crushed
1 teaspoon dijon mustard
Season with black pepper

1. In a small bowl, mix all the dressing ingredients.
2. Put the remaining ingredients in a large salad bowl and toss.
3. Slice open the pitta bread and fill with beef and salad.
4. Pour the dressing over the top and serve.

Poached chicken

2 tablespoons light soy sauce
1 tablespoon Chinese rice wine
2cm piece fresh ginger, sliced
1 tablespoon coriander

6 spring onions, finely sliced
1 litre of chicken stock
4 skinless chicken breasts
Serve with brown rice and vegetables

1. In a large saucepan bring the soy sauce, Chinese rice wine, ginger, coriander, 4 spring onions and chicken stock to a boil.
2. Add the chicken, then reduce the heat and simmer for 12 minutes.
3. Remove from heat and allow chicken to rest in liquid for 5 minutes.
4. Slice chicken thickly and place on serving plate.
5. Pour liquid from saucepan over the chicken and sprinkle the rest of the spring onions over.
6. Serve with rice and vegetables.

Lunch for tomorrow: Chicken salad

1. Heat ½ tablespoon extra virgin olive oil, in a frying pan over a medium heat.
2. Cook the chicken for 8–12 minutes or until cooked.

Recipes for Week 10: Day 4

BREAKFAST

Wheat biscuits, Shredded Wheat or muesli with fruit

560ml milk (soya/rice/oat or skimmed milk)
2–3 wheat biscuits/Shredded Wheat or 240g of muesli, (60g per person)
1 piece of fruit of your choice

Place oats or cereal in a bowl add milk and serve with fruit.

LUNCH

Chicken wrap

4 cooked chicken breasts, cut into strips
4 tortilla organic whole wheat wraps (served hot or cold)
200g mixed salad
4–5 sliced tomatoes

1 red onion, finely chopped
1 yellow pepper, sliced
2 tablespoons of soya/plain yoghurt

1. Heat ½ tablespoon extra virgin olive oil in a frying pan over a medium heat.
2. Cook 4 chicken breasts for 8–12 minutes or until cooked.
3. Place mixed salad, red onion, yellow pepper, tomatoes and chicken in salad bowl and mix well.
4. Place tortilla wraps on plates, add mixture from salad bowl and roll wrap.
5. Drizzle over soya/plain yoghurt.

DINNER

Marlin steaks

For the dressing:
100ml olive oil
2 limes, juiced
1 clove of garlic, crushed
1 tablespoon parsley, of chopped
½ teaspoon dried oregano

1 tablespoon olive oil
4 marlin steaks
Serve with generous amounts of vegetables

1. For the dressing: place the extra virgin olive oil in a mixing bowl and slowly whisk in 70ml of hot water and lime juice.
2. Add the garlic, parsley and oregano and whisk until smooth.
3. Heat the olive oil in a large frying pan on high heat.
4. Add the marlin steaks and cook for 3 minutes each side.
5. Serve with vegetables and drizzle the dressing over the top.

NOTES

Recipes for Week 10: Day 5

Fresh fruit and seeds

8 tablespoons of soya/plain yoghurt
Sprinkle of sunflower or pumpkin seeds
2 pieces of fruit of your choice per person

1. Mix together the soya/plain yoghurt, seeds and fruit
2. Divide into 4 portions.

Your food diary:

Meal	Time	Description
Breakfast:		
Snacks:		
Lunch:		
Snacks:		
Dinner:		
Snacks:		

Tuna and olive salad

175g french beans, topped and tailed
350g fresh tuna steaks
115g baby plum tomatoes, halved
8 anchovy fillets, drained on kitchen paper
25g stoned black olives in brine, drained
Basil leaves, to garnish

For the dressing:
1 tablespoon olive oil
1 garlic clove, crushed
1 tablespoon lemon juice
1 tablespoon basil leaves, shredded

1. Cook the french beans in a small saucepan of boiling water for 5 minutes, or until slightly tender, drain well and keep warm.
2. Season the tuna steaks with black pepper and place tuna on grill rack and cook for 4–5 minutes on each side, or until cooked through.
3. Drain the tuna on kitchen paper and using a knife and fork, flake the tuna into bite size pieces.
4. Mix the tuna, french beans, tomatoes, anchovies and olives into a bowl and keep warm.
5. Mix all the dressing ingredients together. Pour dressing over tuna salad. Garnish with basil and serve.

Baked mediterranean vegetables with ricotta and turkey

1 red pepper, halved and deseeded
1 yellow pepper, halved and deseeded
4 courgettes, finely sliced lengthways
1 aubergine, finely sliced
1 tablespoon olive oil
1 clove garlic, crushed

2 small red onions, finely sliced
4 plum tomatoes, diced
115g fresh basil
200g low fat ricotta cheese or goat's cheese
4 turkey breasts

1. Preheat the oven to 180°C (350°F).
2. Place peppers, skin-side up, in a baking dish and drizzle with a little olive oil and roast for 20 minutes.
3. Remove from oven, cover with foil and allow to cool slightly.
4. Slice flesh into thick strips.
5. Preheat grill to high.
6. In a bowl toss the courgette and aubergine with half the oil and grill vegetables until soft.
7. Heat the remaining oil in a large non-stick frying pan over high heat. Add the garlic and onion and cook until soft.
8. Arrange vegetables, including tomatoes and basil, in layers in a non-stick baking dish.
9. Crumble ricotta cheese over the top and bake for 30 minutes.
10. Grill turkey breasts on medium heat for 8–12 minutes, or until cooked. Keep turning.
11. Serve the turkey with vegetables and ricotta cheese.

Recipes for Week 10: Day 6

BREAKFAST

Omelette

8 eggs (2 eggs per person)
4 tablespoons cold water
8 teaspoons olive oil
400g lean ham
1 courgette, finely sliced
4 spring onions, finely chopped

1. Cook one omelette at a time, beat the eggs with some water in a bowl.
2. Heat the extra virgin olive oil in a non stick pan over a high heat and pour in the eggs. Cook for 2 minutes or until the mixture just begins to set.
3. Place ham and courgette on top of the egg mixture and cook until omelette has set.
4. Sprinkle on the spring onions, fold omelette in half and serve.

LUNCH

Vegetable soup

1 litre vegetable stock
2 carrots, sliced
2 celery sticks, chopped
1 onion, chopped

1 tablespoon fresh parsley, chopped
400g tinned tomatoes
1 tablespoon basil, chopped
1 tablespoon rosemary, finely chopped

1. Bring stock to boil in a large saucepan.
2. Add the carrots, celery, onion, parsley and tomatoes and simmer gently for 30 minutes.
3. Stir through basil and rosemary and season with black pepper.

DINNER

Monkfish delight

16 large raw prawns, peeled
350g cod or haddock fillet, skinned and diced
350g monkfish, diced
2 onions, finely chopped
4 celery sticks, finely chopped
2 tablespoons plain flour
700ml fish stock
1 red pepper, deseeded and chopped
1 green pepper, deseeded and chopped

2 large tomatoes, chopped
1 tablespoon olive oil
1 garlic clove, crushed
½ teaspoon brown sugar
1 teaspoon ground cumin
4 tablespoons parsley, chopped
1 tablespoon fresh coriander, chopped
Dash tabasco sauce
Serve with rice

1. Heat the olive oil in a large saucepan adding the onion, celery and cook for 5 minutes (stir occasionally)
2. Add the garlic and cook for 1 minute.
3. Next, stir in the flour, sugar and cumin and cook for 2 minutes – keep stirring.
4. Gradually stir in the fish stock and bring to boil, stirring constantly.
5. Boil the rice.
6. Add the peppers and tomatoes to the large sausepan and partially cover, reducing the heat to very low and simmer gently for 10 minutes. Stir occasionally.
7. Add the parsley, coriander and tabasco sauce and then gently stir in the fish and peeled prawns.
8. Cover and simmer gently for 5 minutes or until the fish is cooked through and the prawns have changed colour.
9. Gently mix and transfer to serving plates.
10. Serve with rice.

Recipes for Week 10: Day 7

Fruit smoothie

2 large mangos, peeled and chopped
4 bananas, chopped
2 handfuls of raspberries

Blend mangos, bananas and raspberries and serve.

Tuna salad

4 cooked sweet potatoes
4 small tins tuna
1 tablespoon balsamic vinegar
1 tablespoon olive oil

Side salad:
100g of rocket leaves
4 tomatoes, roughly chopped
¼ cucumber, roughly chopped
50g mange-tout
1 red pepper, sliced

1. Preheat oven 190°C (375°F).
2. Cut the sweet potatoes into small chunks and drizzle a tablespoon of exra virgin olive oil and place into oven for 30–40 minutes.
3. Once cooked, allow to cool and place into the fridge for tommorrow's lunch.
4. Place rocket leaves, mange-tout, tomatoes, cucumber and red pepper in a salad bowl and gently mix with balsamic vinegar and olive oil.
5. Serve with the tuna and sweet potatoes.

Garlic lamb

1 tablespoon olive oil
1 onion, chopped
350g lean boneless lamb, diced
600ml vegetable stock
1 orange, Grated rind
1 aubergine, halved lengthways and sliced thinly
4 tomatoes, chopped

115g no-soak dried apricots
1 garlic clove, finely chopped
1 teaspoon clear honey
1 cinnamon stick
1 cm piece ginger, finely chopped
2 tablespoons fresh coriander, chopped
Serve with brown rice

1. Heat the olive oil in a large frying pan over a medium heat.
2. Add the onions and lamb cubes, stirring frequently, for 5 minutes, or until meat is slightly browned all over.
3. Add the garlic, vegetable stock, orange rind and juice, honey, cinnamon stick and ginger and bring to boil.
4. Reduce the heat, cover and simmer for 45 minutes.
5. Add the aubergine, tomatoes and apricots.
6. Cover and cook for a further 45 minutes, or until lamb is tender.
7. Stir in the coriander and season with black pepper.
8. Serve immediately with brown rice.

Lunch for tomorrow: Chicken salad

1. Heat ½ tablespoon extra virgin olive oil, in a frying pan over a medium heat.
2. Cook the chicken for 8–12 minutes or until cooked.

enjoy your food
week 11

Week 11 Overview

DAY	BREAKFAST	LUNCH	DINNER
1	Fresh fruit and seeds	Chicken salad pitta	Fennel and halibut parcels
2	Scrambled egg with wild mushroom	Tuna salad	Mint chicken and lime
3	Muesli and fresh fruit	Yellow split pea soup	Mango and rum snapper
4	Fruit porridge	Salmon salad	Stuffed peppers
5	Fruit salad	Egg salad	Lamb curry with spinach
6	Omelette	Tomato and pepper soup	Hungarian goulash
7	Fruit smoothie	Chicken wrap	Chilli prawn salad

Snack list

- **Fruits:**

  Melon, mango or coconut – 1 to share

  Peach, plum, or kiwi – 1

  Pineapple – 1 to share (I had 2 slices a week)

  Orange or nectarine – 1

  Berries (blackberries, goji, blueberries, raspberries or strawberries) – 2 portions

  Pear – 1

  Banana – 5

  Apple – 5

- **Dr Karg crackers** – 3
- **Crackers/flat breads** – 1
- **Small bowl of muesli** (if really hungry) – 2
- **Yoghurt/soya yoghurt** (four dessert spoons) – 1
- **Nuts** (cashew, pine or occasionally mixed nuts) – 2 to 3 handfuls
- **Soya nuts** – after all training sessions 3 to 4 handfuls
- **Seeds** (pumpkin or sunflower) – 2 to 3 handfuls
- **Pitta bread/wrap with salad and protein filling** – 1

I would roughly snack four to five times a day at random intervals. On average however, I snacked at 10.00am, 12.00pm, 2.30pm and 4.00pm. You can use this as a guide, but you do not need to snack five times a day – just when you need to.

Shopping List
Week 11

Carbohydrates:

1 bag of brown rice
1 bag of couscous
240g of Jordans muesli
560g porridge oats
4 potatoes
1 bag of sunflower seeds
1 bag of pumpkin seeds
4 sweet potatoes
4 organic tortilla wraps
4 wholemeal/brown pitta breads
1 bag of wild rice
Wheat biscuits/Shredded wheat

Dairy and non-dairy alternatives:

8 eggs
200g ricotta/goat's
    cheese
680ml skimmed/Alpro soya/rice/
    oat milk
1.5kg Alpro soya yoghurt

Fish:

8 anchovy fillets
350g cod or haddock
4 marlin steaks
350g monkfish
16 large raw prawns
200g x 4 swordfish steaks
4 tins tuna

Meat:

400g cooked roast beef
8 chicken breasts
400g lean ham
350g boneless lamb
800g rack of lamb
4 turkey breasts

Fruit:

6 apples
1 apricot
8 bananas
1 punnet of blackberries
4 lemons
2 limes
2 mangos
2 oranges
1 peach
1 large pineapple
1 punnet of raspberries
1 watermelon

Vegetables:

2 aubergines
200g baby carrots
4 cooked beetroots
1kg butternut squash
24 black olives
4 carrots
8 celery sticks
8 courgettes
1 cucumber
75g french beans
200g green beans
1 green pepper
2 lettuce
50g mange tout
6 onions
200g peas
150g plum tomatoes
4 red onions
4 red peppers
14 red tomatoes
100g rocket salad
4 shallots
10 spring onions
2 yellow peppers

Herbs:

Basil
Black pepper
Chilli powder
Chives
Cinnamon sticks
Ground coriander
Cumin
Fresh ginger
1 garlic clove
1 green chilli
Mint
Nutmeg
Oregano
Paprika
Parsley
Rosemary
Tarragon
Thyme sprigs
Turmeric

Other:

175g dried apricots
Balsamic vinegar
Chicken stock
Chinese rice vinegar
Cold pressed extra virgin olive oil
Dijon mustard
Fish stock
Honey
Light soy sauce
Plain flour
60ml red wine
Soy sauce
Sugar
Tabasco sauce
400g tinned tomatoes
Tomato puree
Vegetable stock

Snacks:

Fruit
Dr Karg crackers
Crackers/flat breads
Small bowl of muesli
Yoghurt/Alpro soya yoghurt
Nuts (cashew, pine or
    occasionally mixed nuts)
Soya nuts
Seeds (pumpkin or sunflower)

Fruit drinks

1 carton Tropicana/Innocent fruit
drink

Recipes for Week 11: Day 1

Your food diary:

Meal   Time   Description

Breakfast:

Snacks:

Lunch:

Snacks:

Dinner:

Snacks:

Fresh fruit and seeds

8 tablespoons of soya/plain yoghurt
Sprinkle of sunflower or pumpkin seeds
2 pieces of fruit of your choice per person

1. Mix together the soya/plain yoghurt, seeds and fruit
2. Divide into 4 portions.

Chicken salad pitta

4 wholemeal pitta breads (served hot or cold)
4 chicken breasts, cut into small pieces
Generous amount of salad leaves
1 avocado, sliced

1 red pepper, sliced
1 yellow pepper, sliced
2 spring onions, finely chopped
½ tablespoon olive oil

1. Heat olive oil in a frying pan over a medium heat.
2. Cook the chicken for 8–12 minutes, or until cooked.
3. Remove from heat and set aside to rest for 5 minutes.
4. Meanwhile, prepare the salad.

5. Slice open the pitta bread and fill with the chicken and salad.
6. Serve immediately.

Fennel and halibut parcels

4 halibut steaks (175g each)
2 leeks, cut into thin strips
2 courgettes, cut into thin slices
2 carrots, cut into thin slices
1 fennel bulb, halved and cut into thin strips

115g/4oz mushrooms, thinly sliced
4 teaspoons olive oil
4 tablespoons white wine
Serve with vegetables of your choice

1. Preheat oven to 190°C (375°F).
2. Cut out 4 x 30cm/12inch squares of baking paper and spread out on a work surface.
3. Divide the leeks, courgettes, carrots, fennel and mushroom equally between the paper squares.
4. Top each bed of vegetables with halibut steak.
5. Fold up the edges of the paper, but do not seal.
6. Drizzle 1 teaspoon of olive oil and 1 tablespoon of white wine over each fish steak.
7. Fold over the edges of the paper to seal to make a loosely wrapped parcel.

8. Place the parcels on a large baking sheet and bake in oven for 10–15 minutes or until parcels are puffed and fish is cooked.
9. Transfer to plates and serve with vegetables.

Lunch for tomorrow: Tuna salad

1. Preheat oven 190°C (375°F)

TRAIN TO BECOME I 12 WEEK NUTRITION PROGRAMME

BREAKFAST

LUNCH

DINNER

PREPARE

PAGE 120

Recipes for Week 11: Day 2

2. Cut the sweet potatoes into small chunks and drizzle a tablespoon of ex…
3. Place in oven for 30–40 minutes.
4. Once cooked allow to cool then refridgerate for tommorrow's lunch.

Scrambled eggs with wild mushrooms

8 large wild mushrooms
2 teaspoons olive oil
8 eggs
200ml of soya or skimmed milk
1 tablespoon chives, chopped
Ground black pepper

1. Preheat the grill to high heat.
2. Brush mushrooms with olive oil and season with pepper. Grill for about 10 minutes or until tender.

3. Meanwhile, in a bowl, lightly whisk eggs and milk together and lightly season with black pepper.
4. Heat a non-stick frying pan over medium heat and pour in the egg mixture and cook. Keep stirring until the egg is cooked, then stir in chives.
5. Place eggs on the mushrooms and serve.

Tuna salad

4 cooked sweet potatoes
4 small tins tuna
1 tablespoon balsamic vinegar
1 tablespoon olive oil

Side salad:
100g of rocket leaves
4 tomatoes, roughly chopped
¼ cucumber, roughly chopped
50g mange-tout
1 red pepper, sliced

1. Preheat oven 190°C (375°F).
2. Cut the sweet potatoes into small chunks and drizzle a tablespoon of exra virgin olive oil and place into oven for 30–40 minutes.

3. Once cooked, allow to cool and place into the fridge for tommorrow's lunch.
4. Place rocket leaves, mange-tout, tomatoes, cucumber and red pepper in a salad bowl and gently mix with balsamic vinegar and olive.
5. Serve with the tuna and sweet potatoes.

Mint chicken and lime

8 lean, boneless chicken thighs
For the marinade:
3 tablespoons fresh mint, finely chopped
4 tablespoons clear honey
2 tablespoons lime juice

For the sauce:
150g/5.5 oz low fat natural soya/plain yoghurt
1 tablespoon fresh mint, finely chopped
2 teaspoons lime rind, finely grated

1. Mix the honey, mint and lime juice in a large bowl.
2. Add chicken to marinade and evenly coat both sides.
3. Cover with cling film and leave the chicken to refrigerate for at least 30 minutes, longer if possible.

4. Remove the chicken and reserve the marinade. Preheat the grill to medium.
5. Place the chicken on the grill tray and cook under hot grill for 15–18 minutes, or until chicken is tender and cooked. Turn the chicken frequently and keep covering chicken with marinade.
6. Meanwhile, mix all the sauce ingredients together in a bowl.

PAGE 121

BREAKFAST

Recipes for Week 11: Day 3

76. Serve the chicken with the salad and use the remainder marinade for dipping.

Lunch for tomorrow: Yellow split pea soup

Pre-soak 225g of yellow split peas overnight in cold water.

LUNCH

Muesli with fresh fruit

240g muesli (60g per person)
Serving of milk (soya/rice/oat or skimmed milk)
Fruit of your choice, cut into chunks (1 piece of fruit per person)

1. Place muesli in a bowl, add milk.
2. Serve with fruit.

Yellow split pea soup

225g yellow split peas
   (pre-soaked for 12 hours overnight in cold water)
1.5 litres of vegetable stock
1 onion, peeled and sliced

1 sweet potato, peeled and chopped
3 carrots, trimmed, peeled and sliced
Fresh mint
Fresh baby spinach leaves, 4 handfuls

DINNER

1. Drain water from the split peas.
2. Bring the vegetable stock to boil in a large saucepan and add split peas.
3. Simmer for 25 minutes removing any scum on the surface.
4. Add all other vegetables to the saucepan and simmer for a further 15–20 minutes or until vegetables are tender.
5. Remove from heat and allow to cool.
6. Blend soup with food processor or blender.
7. Reheat soup and add the spinach.
8. Serve with a mint garnish.

Mango and rum snapper

2 tablespoons dark rum
50ml white wine
1 tablespoon ginger, finely chopped
1 clove garlic, finely chopped
500g red snapper fillets, cut into 4cm/1.5 inch pieces
1 onion, cut into wedges
1 tablespoon olive oil

2 tablespoons plain flour
2 teaspoons tomato puree
1 red pepper, deseeded and roughly chopped
500ml fish stock
2 large tomatoes, roughly chopped
1 mango, peeled, stoned and roughly chopped
Serve with rice

1. Mix the rum, wine, ginger and garlic in a large, shallow, non-metallic dish and add the fish to marinade.
2. Cover with cling film and leave in the refrigerator to marinate for 30 minutes. Remove using a slotted spoon and

TRAIN TO BECOME I 12 WEEK NUTRITION PROGRAMME

BREAKFAST

LUNCH

DINNER

PREPARE

PAGE 122

Recipes for Week 11: Day 4

reserve the marinade.

3. Boil the rice.
4. Heat the olive oil in a large saucepan, add the onion wedges and cook over for 5 minutes.
5. Stir in the flour and add the tomato puree and red pepper.
6. Gradually stir in the fish stock and the reserved marinade and bring to boil, stirring continuously.
7. Reduce the heat and simmer for a further 3 minutes.
8. Add the fish, tomatoes and mango to the saucepan and cover.
9. Simmer for 8 minutes or until fish is cooked then serve with rice.

Fruit porridge

240g of porridge oats (60g per person)

2-3 apples, chopped

120ml of water or milk (soya/rice/oat or skimmed milk) – enough to cover the oats and apples

1. Slowly bring to the boil the water and/or milk in a sauce pan. Add the oats and chopped apples.
2. Cook for 10 minutes, stirring continuously until thickened. If the mixture becomes too thick, add more water or milk. Serve immediately.

Salmon salad

200g mixed salad leaves

250g cherry tomatoes, halved

Coriander, a handful roughly chopped

For the dressing:

500g soya/plain yoghurt

2 tablespoons coriander, chopped

2-3 spring onions, finely sliced

¼ cucumber, roughly chopped

4 cooked poach salmon fillets, bite-size pieces

2 yellow peppers, sliced

1 garlic clove, finely chopped

4 teaspoons lemon juice

1 teaspoon ground cumin

1. Place all ingredients in a bowl and mix well, season with black pepper.
2. Cover and refrigerate for 5–10 minutes before using. If the sauce is too thick, add some water to thin.
3. Place salad leaves, cherry tomatoes, coriander, spring onions, salmon, cucumber and yellow peppers in a salad bowl and toss.
4. Serve the salad and salmon fillets and pour dressing over the dressing.

Stuffed peppers

4 yellow peppers, halved lengthways and deseeded

1 tablespoon olive oil

1 small onion, finely chopped

2 cloves garlic, crushed

150g baby spinach leaves

1 egg, lightly beaten

40g feta/goat's or mature cheese

2 tablespoons basil

3 tomatoes, chopped

12 button mushrooms, sliced

Serve with salad

1. Preheat oven to 180°C (350°F).
2. Heat the olive oil in a medium frying pan over high heat and add the onions, garlic, tomatoes, mushrooms and

Recipes for Week 11: Day 5

spinach leaves and cook for 5 minutes, or until vegetables are soft.

3. Transfer to a large bowl and allow to cool slightly.
4. Add the egg and 1 tablespoon of water, and stir to combine.
5. Spoon the mixture into peppers and sprinkle the tops with feta/goat's cheese or mature goat's cheese and basil.
6. Place peppers on baking tray and bake for 15–20 minutes, or until peppers are soft and cheese is slightly brown. Serve immediately with rice.

Lunch for tomorrow: Egg salad

1. Boil the 4 eggs for 6½ minutes
2. Place in cold water and allow to cool.
3. Refrigerate overnight.

Fruit salad

8 tablespoons soya yoghurt (2 tablespoons per person)

80g oats

60g sunflower seeds or pumpkin seeds

4-5 pieces of fruit (preferably ones in season)

1. Dice fruit into chunks and divide into 4 portions.

2. Add 2 tablespoons of soya yoghurt in each portion and sprinkle with oats and seeds.

Egg salad

4 baby gem lettuce

200g baby spinach

150g cherry tomatoes, halved

4 shelled hard boiled eggs, cut into quarters

½ cucumber, sliced

1 yellow pepper, deseeded and sliced

For the dressing:

1 tablespoon dijon mustard

1 tablespoon olive oil

2 teaspoons cider vinegar

1 teaspoon water

1. Arrange the lettuce, spinach, tomatoes, yellow pepper, and cucumber on plates.
2. Mix the mustard and water add mix in the olive oil and vinegar into a small bowl.
3. Put the eggs on top of the salad, drizzle with the dressing and serve.

Lamb curry with spinach

800g lean lamb leg, diced

2 tablespoons olive oil

2 onions, finely sliced

Spices:

½ teaspoon cardamon seeds

1 teaspoon ground cinnamon

Recipes for Week 11: Day 6

2 cloves garlic
115g soya/plain yoghurt
1 tin of chopped tomatoes
250g spinach
Fresh coriander, handful

1 tablespoon ga
2 teaspoon tur
Serve with bro

1. Heat olive oil in a large saucepan over high heat and add the onion and garlic.
2. Cook for 5 minutes, or until onion is golden.
3. Add the spices and lamb, mix well and cook for 6–8 minutes, or until lamb begins to cook and change colour.
4. Stir through soya/plain soya/plain yoghurt and tomato.
5. Add spinach and 225ml of water then reduce heat to medium and simmer for 40 minutes, or until meat is tender.
6. Stir through the coriander.
7. Serve with rice.

Fruit smoothie

2 large mangos, peeled and chopped

4 bananas, chopped

2 handfuls of raspberries

Blend mangos, bananas and raspberries and serve.

Tomato and pepper soup

2 red peppers, deseeded and halved
2 tablespoons olive oil
1 large onion, finely sliced
2 cloves of garlic, crushed

1 tablespoon tomato paste
750g tomatoes, roughly chopped
450ml vegetable stock
Basil, handful

1. Preheat oven 180°C (350°F).
2. Place red peppers in baking tray, skin side up and drizzle with half the olive oil.
3. Roast for 25 minutes, or until soft and remove from oven. Allow to cool slightly, then roughly chop.
4. Heat the rest of the oil in a large saucepan, over medium heat.
5. Add the onion and cook until soft.
6. Add garlic and tomato paste and cook for 2 minutes, stirring continuously.
7. Add red pepper, tomato and stock, cover and simmer for 15 minutes.
8. Allow the soup to cool slightly, and gently stir.
9. Season with basil and serve.

Hungarian goulash

800g lean braising steak
400g chopped tomatoes tinned

Herbs:
1 bay leaf

Recipes for Week 11: Day 7

Your food diary:

Meal   Time   Description

Breakfast:

Snacks:

Lunch:

Snacks:

Dinner:

Snacks:

2 onions, finely chopped

220g mushrooms, sliced

2 green peppers, deseeded and diced

tablespoons paprika

280g very low fat natural fromage frais

teaspoon caraway seeds

Florets of broccoli

125g of peas

Marjoram, pinch

Thyme, pinch

2 level

¼ level

Serve with brown rice and vegetables

1. Preheat oven to 150C (300°F).
2. Place onions and tomatoes in pan and cook until onions are soft.
3. Add the mushrooms and peppers and cook for a further 5 minutes.
4. Cut the steak into strips and place in a casserole dish, adding the herbs and tomato mixture.

5. Cover and cook for 1 hour 30 minutes to 1 hour 45 minutes.
6. Beat the fromage frais until smooth and pour over the casserole dish before serving.
7. Serve with the vegetables and brown rice.

Omelette

8 eggs (2 eggs per person)

4 tablespoons of cold water

8 teaspoons of extra virgin olive oil cold pressed

400g lean ham

1 courgette, finely sliced

4 spring onions, finely chopped

1. Cook one omelette at a time, beat the eggs with some water in a bowl.
2. Heat the extra virgin olive oil in a non stick pan over a high heat and pour in the eggs. Cook for 2 minutes or until the mixture just begins to set.
3. Place ham and courgette on top of the egg mixture and cook until omelette has set.
4. Sprinkle on the spring onions, fold omelette in half and serve.

Chicken wrap

4 cooked chicken breasts, cut into strips

4 tortilla organic whole wheat wraps (served hot or cold)

200g mixed salad

4–5 sliced tomatoes

1 red onion, finely chopped

1 yellow pepper, sliced

2 tablespoons of soya/plain yoghurt

1. Heat ½ tablespoon extra virgin olive oil in a frying pan over a medium heat.
2. Cook 4 chicken breasts for 8–12 minutes or until cooked.
3. Place mixed salad, red onion, yellow pepper, tomatoes and chicken in salad bowl and mix well.
4. Place tortilla wraps on plates, add mixture from salad bowl and roll wrap.
5. Drizzle over yoghurt.

Chilli prawn salad

1 tablespoon olive oil

1cm ginger, peeled and finely chopped

2 cloves garlic, finely chopped

2 fresh red chillies, deseeded and finely sliced

For the salad:

1 cos lettuce, tear into pieces

3–4 spring onions, finely sliced

4 large tomatoes, sliced

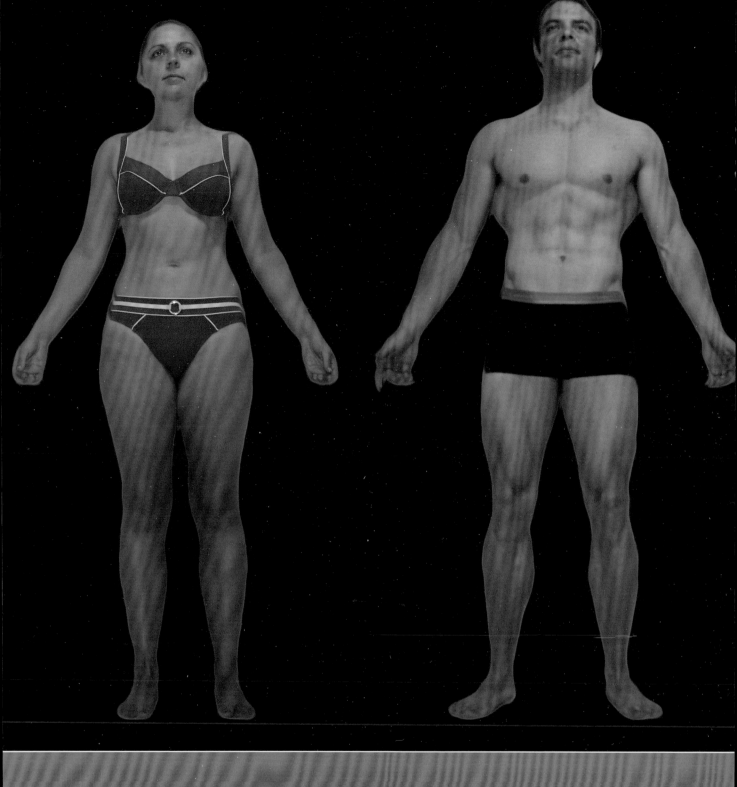

enjoy your food
week 12

Week 12 Overview

DAY	BREAKFAST	LUNCH	DINNER
1	Fresh fruit and seeds	Tuna salad	Jambalaya
2	Fruit smoothie	Smoked salmon pitta	Grilled sea bass with fresh vegetables
3	Muesli and fresh fruit	Sweet potato and bean salad	Vegetable Thai curry
4	Fruit porridge	Chicken salad pitta	Monkfish salad
5	Wheat biscuits/Shredded Wheat or muesli with a piece of fruit	Butternut squash and coriander soup	Baked rainbow trout
6	Fruit salad	Mackerel salad	Lamb shanks
7	Omelette	Tuna and olive salad	Butternut squash and lentil stew

Snack list

- **Fruits:**

  Melon, mango or coconut – 1 to share

  Peach, plum, or kiwi – 1

  Pineapple – 1 to share (I had 2 slices a week)

  Orange or nectarine – 1

  Berries (blackberries, goji, blueberries, raspberries or strawberries) – 2 portions

  Pear – 1

  Banana – 5

  Apple – 5
- **Dr Karg crackers** – 3
- **Crackers/flat breads** – 1
- **Small bowl of muesli** (if really hungry) – 2
- **Yoghurt/soya yoghurt** (four dessert spoons) – 1
- **Nuts** (cashew, pine or occasionally mixed nuts) – 2 to 3 handfuls
- **Soya nuts** – after all training sessions 3 to 4 handfuls
- **Seeds** (pumpkin or sunflower) – 2 to 3 handfuls
- **Pitta bread/wrap with salad and protein filling** – 1

I would roughly snack four to five times a day at random intervals. On average however, I snacked at 10.00am, 12.00pm, 2.30pm and 4.00pm. You can use this as a guide, but you do not need to snack five times a day – just when you need to.

Shopping List

Week 12

Carbohydrates:

75g brown basmati rice
50g wholegrain brown barley
1 bag of brown rice
400g kidney beans
225g lentils
25g millet seeds
250g of Jordans muesli
125g new potatoes
1 bag of pine nuts
400g pinto beans
560g porridge oats
3 potatoes
1 bag of sunflower seeds
1 bag pumpkin seeds
12 sweet potatoes
8 wholemeal or brown pitta breads
Wheat biscuits/Shredded wheat

Dairy and non-dairy alternatives:

8 eggs
60g feta/goat's cheese
1880ml skimmed/Alpro soya/ rice/ oat milk
1.7kg Alpro soya soghurt

Fish:

8 anchovy fillets
225g fresh mackerel
600g monkfish tail
4 salmon fillets
8 king size prawns
4 rainbow trout
4 sea bass fillets
4 pack of smoked salmon
4 small tins tuna
350g tuna steaks

Meat:

8 chicken breasts
8 chicken thighs
100g raw chorizo
100g raw garlic sausage
2kg lamb shank
400g lean ham

Fruit:

8 apples
2 apricots
10 bananas
1 lime
3 lemons
1 mango
2 oranges
2 peaches
1 large pineapple
1 small packet of raisins
1 punnet of raspberries
1 watermelon

Vegetables:

3 avocados
100g baby corn
2 bags of baby spinach
1.4kg butternut squash
25g black olives
250g cherry tomatoes
5 carrots
4 celery sticks
3 courgettes
½ cucumber
175g french beans
2 green peppers
2 lettuces
50g mange tout
1 marrow
150g mushrooms
6 onions
115g plum tomatoes
1 red onion
5 red peppers
8 red tomatoes
100g rocket salad
1 shallot
100g sugar snap peas
10 spring onions
2 yellow peppers

Herbs:

Basil
2 bay leaves
Black pepper
Coriander
Ground coriander
Ground cumin
Dill
1 garlic clove
Fresh ginger
1 lemongrass stalk
Nutmeg
Oregano
Paprika
Parsley
2 red chillies
Rosemary
Thyme
Turmeric

Other:

Balsamic vinegar
Chicken stock
400ml coconut milk
Cold pressed extra virgin olive oil
Dijon mustard
Plain flour
400g tinned plum tomatoes
vegetable stock
115ml white wine
White wine vinegar

Snacks:

Fruit
Dr Karg crackers
Crackers/flat breads
Small bowl of muesli
Yoghurt/Alpro soya yoghurt
Nuts (cashew, pine or occasionally mixed nuts)
Soya nuts
Seeds (pumpkin or sunflower)

Fruit drinks

1 carton Tropicana/Innocent fruit drink

Recipes for Week 12: Day 1

Your food diary:

Meal	Time	Description
Breakfast:		
Snacks:		
Lunch:		
Snacks:		
Dinner:		
Snacks:		

Fresh fruit and seeds

8 tablespoons of soya/plain yoghurt
Sprinkle of sunflower or pumpkin seeds
2 pieces of fruit of your choice per person

1. Mix together the soya/plain yoghurt, seeds and fruit
2. Divide into 4 portions.

Tuna salad

4 cooked sweet potatoes
4 small tinned tuna
1 tablespoon balsamic vinegar
1 tablespoon olive oil

Side salad:
100g of rocket leaves
4 tomatoes, roughly chopped
¼ cucumber, roughly chopped
50g mange-tout
1 red pepper, sliced

1. Preheat oven 190°C (375°F).
2. Cut the sweet potatoes into small chunks and drizzle over a tablespoon of exra virgin olive oil and place into oven for 30–40 minutes.
3. Once cooked, allow to cool and place into the fridge for tommorrow's lunch.
4. Place rocket leaves, mangetout, tomatoes, cucumber and red pepper in a salad bowl and gently mix with balsamic vinegar and olive oil.
5. Serve with the tuna and sweet potatoes.

Jambalaya

4 skinless, boneless chicken thighs, halved
1 tablespoon flour
1 onion, peeled and finely chopped
½ red pepper, deseeded and chopped
½ green pepper, deseeded and chopped
50g wholegrain brown barley,
 soaked in boiling water and drained
230g tinned chopped tomatoes
500ml chicken stock
100g raw garlic sausage, roughly chopped
 and lightly dry-fried

100g raw chorizo, roughly chopped
 and lightly dry-fried
75g brown basmati rice
8 king size prawns, peeled
1 tablespoon olive oil
1 clove garlic, peeled and finely chopped
1 teaspoon fresh thyme leaves
1 red chilli, deseeded and roughly chopped
25g millet seeds, dry-fried until they 'pop'

1. Dust the chicken in the flour.
2. Heat the olive oil in a large non-stick frying pan and add the onion, garlic, red and green pepper, thyme and chilli to the pan and cook over medium heat until onion is soft.
3. Add the barley, tomatoes, chicken stock and bring to boil.
4. Add the chicken and sausages and lower the heat and stir in the rice and millet.
5. Cover and cook for 20 minutes or until the rice is almost tender.
6. Remove the lid and simmer for a further 10 minutes.
7. Stir in the prawns and cook for a further 5 minutes.
8. Serve on warm plates and enjoy!

Recipes for Week 12: Day 2

BREAKFAST

Fruit smoothie

4 tablespoons nut and seed muesli
1200ml milk (soya/rice/oat or skimmed milk)
2 bananas
2 apricots
2 peaches

1. Mix the muesli and milk in a blender until nearly smooth.
2. Add the bananas, peaches and apricots and blend until completely smooth.
3. If the smoothie is too thick, add more water.

LUNCH

Smoked salmon pitta

4 wholemeal pitta breads (served hot or cold)
Smoked salmon
Goat's or cheddar cheese (small serving per person)
2 spring onions, finely sliced

200g baby spinach
4 large tomatoes, sliced into quarters
1 red pepper, finely sliced

1. Slice open pitta bread and spread the goat cheese thinly across one side.
2. Add the smoke salmon and sprinkle over the spring onions.
3. Serve with spinach, tomatoes and red pepper.

DINNER

Grilled sea bass with fresh vegetables

4 fillets sea bass (150g each)
300g tinned lentils, drained and rinsed
 (try and use fresh lentils if you have time)
Serve with broccoli and other green vegetables

For the marinade:
3 garlic cloves, peeled and crushed
2 tablespoon fresh parsley, chopped
2 tablespoon water
Black pepper
3 teaspoons dried oregano
4 teaspoons olive oil
4 tablespoons lemon juice

1. To make the marinade: mix the oregano, garlic, olive oil, lemon juice, black pepper, water and parsley.
2. Wash the fish fillet and pat dry with kitchen towel. Then place on plate and spoon over half the marinade. Cover and refrigerate for 1–2 hours.
3. Preheat the grill to high.
4. Grill the fillet's skin side down for 5–6 minutes until just cooked through – the flesh should be white.
5. Meanwhile, warm the lentils with the marinade.
6. Spoon onto warm plates and place sea bass on top.
7. Serve with fresh vegetables.

PREPARE

Lunch for tomorrow: Sweet potato and bean salad

1. Preheat oven 190°C (375°F).
2. Cut the sweet potatoes into small chunks and drizzle over a tablespoon of exra virgin olive oil.
3. Put into a hot oven for 30–40 minutes.
4. Once cooked and cooled, place into the fridge for tommorow's lunch.

Recipes for Week 12: Day 3

BREAKFAST

Muesli with fresh fruit

240g muesli (60g per person)
Serving of milk (soya/rice/oat or skimmed milk)
Fruit of your choice, cut into chunks (1 piece of fruit per person)

1. Place muesli in a bowl, add milk.
2. Serve with fruit.

LUNCH

Sweet potato and bean salad

4 cooked sweet potatoes

4 eggs

2 avocados, stoned and peeled

400g tinned kidney beans

400g tinned pinto beans

1 small red onion, finely sliced

Coriander, large handful chopped

250g cherry tomatoes, halved

1. Preheat oven 190°C (375°F)
2. Boil 4 eggs for 6½ minutes, then place in cold water to cool slightly.
3. Cut the sweet potatoes into small chunks and drizzle a tablespoon of exra virgin olive oil and place into oven for 30–40 minutes.
4. Slice avocados and place in bowl with beans, sweet potatoes, onions, coriander and tomatoes.
5. Mix with the olive oil, lime juice, chilli and cumin in a small bowl.
6. Once eggs have cooled but are still warm, peel off the shells and cut into quarters.
7. Toss the salad with the dressing, place the eggs on top and serve.

DINNER

Vegetable thai curry

400ml tin coconut milk

½ teaspoon ground coriander

½ teaspoon ground cumin

2 cm fresh ginger, peeled and sliced

1 stalk of lemon grass, cut into 2 cm pieces

100g sugar snap peas

1 red pepper, deseeded and sliced

1 yellow pepper, deseeded and sliced

100g baby corn, halved lengthways

2 courgettes, trimmed and chopped

2 spring onions, trimmed and finely sliced

Basil leaves to garnish

Serve with brown rice

1. Heat coconut milk in a wok or large frying pan over high heat.
2. Add ground coriander, ground cumin, ginger, and lemon grass and cook for 2–3 minutes.
3. Add the peas, peppers, baby corn, courgettes and cook for a further 3–4 minutes or until vegetables are just cooked.
4. Garnish with spring onions and basil.
5. Serve with brown rice.

PREPARE

Lunch for tomorrow: Chicken salad pitta

1. Heat ½ tablespoon extra virgin olive oil in a frying pan over a medium heat.
2. Cook the chicken for 8–12 minutes or until cooked.

Recipes for Week 12: Day 4

Fruit porridge

240g of porridge oats (60g per person)

2-3 apples, chopped

120ml of water or milk (soya/rice/oat or skimmed milk) –
  enough to cover the oats and apples

1. Slowly bring to the boil the water and/or milk in a sauce pan.
2. Add the oats and chopped apples.
3. Cook for 10 minutes, stirring continuously until thickened. If the mixture becomes too thick, add more water or milk. Serve immediately.

Chicken salad pitta

4 wholemeal pitta breads (served hot or cold)

4 chicken breasts, cut into small pieces

Generous amount of salad leaves

1 avocado, sliced

1 red pepper, sliced

1 yellow pepper, sliced

2 spring onions, finely chopped

½ tablespoon olive oil

1. Heat olive oil in a frying pan over a medium heat.
2. Cook the chicken for 8–12 minutes, or until cooked.
3. Remove from heat and set aside to rest for 5 minutes.
4. Meanwhile, prepare the salad.
5. Slice open the pitta bread and fill with the chicken and salad. Serve immediately.

Monkfish salad

600g monkfish tail, wash and remove membrane

1 tablespoon olive oil

2 teaspoons rosemary, chopped

6 plum tomatoes

For the salad:

2 teaspoons olive oil

2 tablespoons pine nuts

1 garlic clove, peeled and sliced

450g baby spinach

2 tablespoons raisins

1 lemon, juice

1. Preheat the oven to 220°C (425°F). Mix the olive oil and the rosemary in a small bowl, season with pepper and lightly coat the fish with this mixture.
2. Place the fish in a roasting tin with the tomatoes and bake in the oven for 20 minutes or until the fish is firm and white.
3. Meanwhile, heat the olive oil in a large frying pan adding the pine nuts and garlic and cook until golden.
4. Add the spinach leaves, raisins and lemon juice a handful at a time.
5. Cut the fish from either side of the central bone.
6. Serve with spinach and cooking juices.

Lunch for tomorrow: Butternut squash and coriander soup

1. In a large saucepan, bring chicken stock to boil.
2. Add the vegetables and spices and bring back to boil.
3. Reduce heat and simmer for 20 minutes or until vegetables are soft.
4. Allow to cool and blend in a food processor.
5. Refrigerate overnight.

Recipes for Week 12: Day 5

Wheat biscuits, Shredded Wheat or muesli with fruit

560ml milk (soya/rice/oat or skimmed milk)

2-3 wheat biscuits/Shredded Wheat or 240g muesli, (60g per person)

1 piece of fruit of your choice

Place oats or cereal in a bowl add milk and serve with fruit.

Your food diary:

Meal	Time	Description
Breakfast:		
Snacks:		
Lunch:		
Snacks:		
Dinner:		
Snacks:		

Butternut squash and coriander soup

900ml chicken stock

1kg butternut squash, peeled and roughly chopped

1 onion, roughly chopped

2 carrots, roughly chopped

2 celery sticks, roughly chopped

1 garlic clove, finely chopped

1 teaspoon paprika

½ teaspoon turmeric

½ teaspoon ground coriander

½ teaspoon ground nutmeg

1. In a large saucepan, bring chicken stock to boil.
2. Add vegetables and spices and bring back to boil.
3. Reduce heat and simmer for 20 minutes, or until vegetables are soft.
4. Allow to cool and then blend.
5. Reheat soup and serve.

Baked rainbow trout

4 rainbow trout, gutted

2 oranges, sliced with skin on

2.5cm fresh ginger, cut into slices

3 sweet potatoes, cut into small chunks

1 marrow, remove skin and cut into small chunks

2 garlic cloves, crushed

40g goat's/mature cheddar cheese

Serve with salad

3 teaspoons dried basil

1 tablespoon olive oil

For the dressing:

1 tablespoon fresh dill, finely chopped

250g plain soya/plain yoghurt

1 garlic clove, crushed

1 teaspoon balsamic vinegar

1. Pre heat oven to 190°C (375°F).
2. Place the sweet potatoes, marrow, garlic and dried basil in a large baking dish and drizzle with olive oil
3. Bake for 30–40 minutes or until cooked.
4. Add the feta/goat's cheese or mature cheddar cheese in the last 5–8 minutes.
5. Meanwhile, prepare the dressing by mixing all the dressing ingredients in a small bowl, then place in refrigerator.
6. Preheat the grill to medium.
7. Place 2 orange slices in each trout and sprinkle the ginger evenly between the 4 fish.
8. Grill the fish for 12–14 minutes, turning occasionally.
9. Arrange the grilled trout on a bed of salad with the sweet potatoes and marrow.
10. Drizzle over the dressing and serve.

Recipes for Week 12: Day 6

Fruit salad

8 tablespoons soya yoghurt (2 tablespoons per person)
80g oats
60g sunflower seeds or pumpkin seeds
4–5 pieces of fruit (preferably ones in season)

1. Dice fruit into chunks and divide into 4 portions.
2. Add 2 tablespoons of soya yoghurt in each portion and sprinkle with oats and seeds.

Your food diary:

Meal	Time	Description
Breakfast:		
Snacks:		
Lunch:		
Snacks:		
Dinner:		
Snacks:		

Mackerel salad

125g new potatoes, scrubbed and diced
225g fresh mackerel fillets
  remove skin and cut into bite-size pieces
1.2 litres, water,
1 eating apple, cored and diced

1 shallot, thinly sliced
3 tablespoons, white wine vinegar,
¼ teaspoon, dijon mustard,
2 tablespoons low fat soya/plain yoghurt
¼ cucumber, thinly sliced

1. Steam the potatoes over a saucepan of simmering water for 10 minutes.
2. Bring water to boil in another saucepan, then reduce the heat to just simmering and add the mackerel pieces, bay leaf and lemon.
3. Poach for 3 minutes, or until flesh is opaque.
4. Remove fish from saucepan and transfer to serving dish.
5. Drain the potatoes and transfer to a large bowl.
6. Mix the apple and shallot, then spoon the mixture over the mackerel.
7. Mix together the vinegar, olive oil, sugar and mustard in bowl and whisk thoroughly.
8. Pour the dressing over potato mixture, cover and chill in the refrigerator for up to 6 hours.
9. Spread the soya/plain yoghurt over salad and place the cucumbers on top.
10. Sprinkle with fresh chives and serve.

Lamb shanks

2 tablespoons olive oil
2kg lamb shanks on the bone
2 onions, chopped
1 celery stick
115ml white wine

675ml chicken stock
2 cloves garlic
2 bay leaves
2 tablespoons parsley
1 tablespoon lemon, zest

Serve with vegetables of your choice and new potatoes

1. Preheat oven to 160°C (325°F).
2. Heat a large heavy-based saucepan over a high heat.
3. Coat the lamb shanks with olive oil and cook in saucepan, turning occasionally, for 10 minutes, or until well-browned then remove to a plate.
4. Add the garlic, onion, and celery to the pan and cook for 5 minutes, or until soft.
5. Next add the wine, stock, lemon zest, parsley and bay leaves and bring to boil.
6. Gently place the lamb shanks in a casserole dish and add the mixture from the pan.
7. Cover with foil and cook in oven for 1–2 hours, or until meat begins to fall off the bone.
8. Garnish with parsley and serve with steamed vegetables and new potatoes.

Recipes for Week 12: Day 7

BREAKFAST

Omelette

8 eggs (2 eggs per person)
4 tablespoons water, cold
8 teaspoons olive oil
400g lean ham
1 courgette, finely sliced
4 spring onions, finely chopped
Parsley to garnish

1. Cook omelette for one person at a time. Beat the eggs with water in a bowl.
2. Heat the olive oil in a non stick pan over a high heat.
3. Pour in eggs and cook for 2 minutes or until mixture just begins to set.
4. Place ham and courgette on top of the egg mixture and cook until omelette has set.
5. Sprinkle over parsley and spring onions.
6. Fold omelette in half and serve. Repeat process.

LUNCH

Tuna and olive salad

175g french beans, topped and tailed
350g fresh tuna steaks
115g baby plum tomatoes, halved
8 anchovy fillets, drained on kitchen paper
25g stoned black olives in brine, drained
Fresh basil leaves to garnish

For the dressing:
1 tablespoon olive oil
1 garlic clove, crushed
1 tablespoon lemon juice
1 tablespoon basil leaves, shredded

1. Cook the french beans in a small saucepan of boiling water for 5 minutes, or until slightly tender, drain well and keep warm.
2. Season the tuna steaks with black pepper and place tuna on grill rack and cook for 4–5 minutes on each side, or until cooked through.
3. Drain the tuna on kitchen paper and using a knife and fork, flake the tuna into bite size pieces.
4. Mix the tuna, french beans, tomatoes, anchovies and olives into a bowl and keep warm.
5. Mix all the dressing ingredients together. Pour dressing over tuna salad. Garnish with basil and serve.

DINNER

Butternut squash and lentil stew

225g lentils
2 onions, peeled and finely chopped
750ml vegetable stock
3 carrots, peeled and chopped
½ butternut squash, peeled, deseeded and chopped

1 sweet potato, peeled and chopped
3 small white potatoes, peeled and chopped
1 celery stalk, trimmed and chopped
50g frozen or fresh peas

1. Soak the lentils in cold water for 20 minutes, rinse and drain.
2. Bring the vegetable stock to boil in a large saucepan.
3. Next, add the onions, lentils, carrots, squash, sweet potato and white potatoes and bring back to boil.
4. Lower the heat and simmer for 10–20 minutes.
5. Add the celery and simmer for a further 5 minutes.
6. Add the peas and simmer for a couple more minutes.
7. Serve in bowls and enjoy!

Relishes and dressings

houmous

1 large can chickpeas, drained
2 cloves garlic
2–3 tablespoons olive oil
1 dessertspoon tahini (sesame seed spread)

tzatziki

1 clove garlic, crushed
200g yogurt
¼ cucumber, finely grated
½ red onion, finely chopped
1 tablespoon parsley, chopped
1 tablespoon mint, chopped

avocado relish

2 avocados, peeled and chopped
1 tablespoon lime juice
½ small red onion, finely cut
2 tomatoes, chopped

relish

1 bunch fresh parsley
6 anchovy fillets
Zest of 2 lemons, grated
115ml lemon juice
60ml olive oil

mint dressing

150g yoghurt
2 tablespoon mint, chopped
½ tablespoon olive oil
2 tablespoon lemon juice

basil dressing

1 tablespoon olive oil
1 clove garlic, crushed
1 tablespoon lemon juice
1 tablespoon basil leaves, shredded

Salad dressing

4 tablespoons yoghurt
¼ cucumber, grated
1 tablespoon olive oil
1 tablespoon balsamic vinegar
2 teaspoons black pepper
2 teaspoons dried dill

nutty delight dressing

3 tablespoons olive oil
3 tablespoons yoghurt
sprinkle of pine nuts
½ tablespoon balsamic vinegar
black pepper

mustard dressing

1 tablespoon dijon mustard
1 tablespoon olive oil
2 teaspoons cider vinegar
1 teaspoon water

dill dressing

1 tablespoon fresh dill, chopped
250g yoghurt
1 clove garlic, crushed
1 teaspoon balsamic vinegar

dressing

2 tablespoon olive oil
1 tablespoon balsamic vinegar
1 clove garlic, crushed
1 teaspoon dijon mustard
black pepper

ginger dressing for the wok

2 tablespoons light soy sauce
2 teaspoons lime juice
1 teaspoon ginger, grated

spicy dressing

2 tablespoons lime juice
1 tablespoon fish sauce
1 tablespoon light soy sauce
1 clove garlic, crushed
1 red chilli, de-seeded and chopped

coriander and yoghurt dressing

500g yoghurt
2 tablespoons coriander, chopped
1 clove garlic, finely chopped
4 teaspoons lemon juice
1 teaspoon ground cumin

spicy dressing

1 red chilli, finely sliced
½ teaspoon ground cumin
1 tablespoon lime juice

Shopping List
Week 1

Carbohydrates:

1 bag of brown rice
480g of Jordans muesli
1 bag of pine nuts
8 wholemeal/brown pitta breads
240g porridge oats
4 jacket potatoes
1 bag of sunflower seeds
1 bag of pumpkin seeds
9 sweet potatoes
4 organic tortilla wraps
Wheat biscuits/Shredded wheat

Dairy and non-dairy alternatives:

350g mature cheddar/goat's
   hard cheese
8 eggs
40g feta/goat's cheese
1 light soft cheese /
   soft goat's cheese
680ml skimmed/Alpro soya/rice/
oat milk
2kg Alpro soya/plain yoghurt

Fish:

8 anchovy fillets
4 mackerel fillets
4 salmon fillets
1 pack of smoked salmon
4 small tuna cans
350g tuna steaks

Meat:

4 200g beef steaks
8 chicken breasts
400g lean ham
8 turkey breasts
1.4kg rack of veal

Fruit:

6 apples
12 bananas
1 punnet of blueberries
2 lemons
2 mangos
1 orange
1 large pineapple
1 punnet of raspberries

Vegetables:

1 avocado
100g baby corn
2 bags of baby spinach
25g black olives
3 butternut squash
5 carrots
2 celery sticks
2 courgettes
1 cucumber
175g french beans
2 leeks
4 lettuces
265g mange tout
150g mushrooms
1 onion
115g plum tomatoes
5 red onions
5 red peppers
20 red tomatoes
100g rocket salad
26 spring onions
1 bag of sweet corn
2 yellow peppers

Herbs:

Basil
Black pepper
Chinese five spice
Coriander
Cumin
Dill
Fresh ginger
1 garlic clove
Green chilli
Ground coriander
Mint
Nutmeg
Paprika
Turmeric

Other:

Balsamic vinegar
Chicken stock
Cold pressed extra virgin olive oil
Ginger wine
Soy sauce
Tandoori paste
Tomato puree

Snacks:

Fruit
Dr Karg crackers/flat breads
Small bowl of muesli
Alpro soya yoghurt
Nuts (cashew, pine or
     occasionally mixed nuts)
Soya nuts
Seeds (pumpkin or sunflower)

Fruit drinks:

1 carton Tropicana/Innocent fruit
drink

Shopping List
Week 2

Carbohydrates:

1 bag of brown rice
75g butternut beans
400g cannellini beans
50g tinned chickpeas
250g couscous
475g kidney beans
490g Jordans muesli
10 new potatoes
1 bag of pine nuts
400g pinto beans
8 wholemeal or brown
  pitta breads
320g porridge oats
1 bag of sunflower seeds
1 bag of pumpkin seeds
8 sweet potatoes
4 bags of wild rice
Wheat biscuits/Shredded wheat

Dairy and non-dairy alternatives:

20 eggs
40g feta/goat's cheese
1520ml skimmed/Alpro soya/rice
oat milk
2kg Alpro soya yoghurt

Fish:

8 anchovy fillets
4 plaice fillets
4 salmon fillets
1 pack of smoked salmon
200g (x 4) swordfish
4 small tuna cans
750g tuna steaks

Meat:

400g cooked roast beef
6 lamb chops
400g lean ham
8 turkey breasts
1.4kg rack of veal

Fruit:

7 apples
2 apricots
6 bananas
1 punnet of blueberries
2 lemons
1 lime
1 orange
2 peaches
1 large pineapple
1 punnet of raspberries

Vegetables:

2 avocados
4 baby aubergines
2 bags of baby spinach
4 cooked beetroot
25g black olives
175g broccoli
250g cherry tomatoes
1 butternut squash
6 carrots
4 celery sticks
5 courgettes
1 cucumber
175g french beans
2 leeks
3 lettuces
50g mange tout
8 mushrooms
5 onions
135g plum tomatoes
8 red onions
3 red peppers
10 red tomatoes
100g rocket salad
8 spring onions
4 shallots
1 bag of sweet corn
1 yellow pepper

Herbs:

Basil
Black pepper
Cayenne pepper
Chilli powder
Chinese five spice
Chives
Coriander
Cumin
Fresh ginger
Garam masala
1 garlic clove
Ground coriander
Ground pepper
Mint
Parsley
1 red chilli
Rosemary
Turmeric

Other:

Balsamic vinegar
Chicken stock
Chilli sauce
Cold pressed extra virgin olive oil
Corn flour
Dijon mustard
Ginger wine
Soy sauce
Sesame oil
Tandoori paste
400g tinned tomatoes
Tomato puree
Vegetable stock
White wine vinegar
Wholegrain mustard

Snacks:

Fruit
Dr Karg Crackers
Crackers/flat breads
Small bowl of muesli
Yoghurt/Alpro soya yoghurt
Nuts (cashew, pine or now and
     again mixed nuts)
Soya nuts
Seeds (pumpkin or sunflower)

Fruit drinks:

1 carton Tropicana/Innocent fruit
drink

Shopping List
Week 3

Carbohydrates:

1 bag of brown rice
240g of Jordans muesli
10 new potatoes
1 bag of pine nuts
8 wholemeal or brown pitta breads
560g porridge oats
1 bag of rice noodles
1 bag of sunflower and pumpkin seeds
4 organic tortilla wraps
6 sweet potatoes
Wheat biscuits/Shredded wheat

3 lettuces
450g mange tout
11 onions
225g frozen peas
4 plum tomatoes
3 red onions
4 red peppers
14 red tomatoes
100g rocket salad
13 spring onions
4 yellow peppers

Dairy and non-dairy alternatives:

12 eggs
680ml skimmed/Alpro soya/rice/oat milk
1.7kg Alpro soya yoghurt

Fish:

200g 4 x cod fillets
4 lemon sole
175g tuna steaks

Meat:

400g lean minced beef
12 chicken breasts
800g chicken thigh fillets
400g lean ham
450g pork fillets
4 turkey breasts
1.4kg rack of veal

Fruit:

3 apples
2 apricots
8 bananas
1 lemon
2 limes
3 oranges
2 mangos
1 melon
1 large pineapple
1 punnet of raspberries

Vegetables:

2 avocados
115g baby corn
4 baby gem lettuce
600g baby spinach
400g bamboo shoots
175g broccoli
200g button mushrooms
300g cherry tomatoes
2 butternut squash
8 carrots
7 celery sticks
2 courgettes
1 cucumber
3 leeks

Herbs:

Basil
Black pepper
Coriander
Cumin
Dill
Fresh ginger
1 garlic clove
1 lemon thyme sprig
Nutmeg
Parsley
Rosemary
Turmeric

Other:

Balsamic vinegar
Beef stock
Chicken stock
Chinese white wine vinegar
Cold pressed extra virgin olive oil
Corn flour
Plain flour
Dark soy sauce
115ml red wine
Soy sauce
400g tinned tomatoes
Vegetable stock
115ml white wine
White wine vinegar

Snacks:

Fruits
Dr Karg crackers
Crackers/flat breads
Small bowl of muesli
Yoghurt/Alpro soya yoghurt
Nuts (cashew, pine or now and again mixed nuts)
Soya nuts
Seeds (pumpkin or sunflower)

Fruit drinks:

1 carton Tropicana/Innocent fruit drink

Shopping List
Week 4

Carbohydrates:

400g baked potatoes
1 bag of brown rice
810g kidney beans
240g of Jordans muesli
400g pinto beans
400g new potatoes
520g porridge oats
1 bag of rice noodles
1 bag of sunflower and pumpkin seeds
4 organic tortilla wraps
1 bag of sesame seeds
8 sweet potatoes
Wheat biscuits/Shredded wheat

7 onions
3 pak choi
4 parsnips
50g frozen peas
115g plum tomatoes
3 red onions
7 red peppers
11 + 750g red tomatoes
100g rocket salad
200g savoy cabbage
1 turnip
1 yellow pepper

Dairy and non-dairy alternatives:

12 Eggs
680ml skimmed/Alpro soya/rice/oat milk
1.7kg Alpro soya yoghurt

Fish:

8 anchovy fillets
4 x 200g cod fillets
4 cooked mackerel
1150g tuna steaks
4 tins tuna
4 whole trout

Meat:

4 chicken breasts
1 large whole chicken
800g pork fillet
400g lean ham
800g lamb chop
800g pork fillet
4 turkey breasts

Fruit:

12 apples
8 bananas
1 punnet of blueberries
5 lemon
2 limes
2 mangos
1 melon
1 punnet of raspberries
1 punnet of strawberries

Vegetables:

4 aubergines
2 avocados
8 asparagus
500g raw beetroot
16 + 25g black olives
500g cherry tomatoes
2 carrots
2 celery sticks
4 courgettes
½ cucumber
50g french beans
175g green beans
2 lettuces
50g mange tout

Herbs:

Basil
1 Bay leaf
Black pepper
Black peppercorns
2 cardamom pods
Chilli powder
Chives
Cinnamon
Coriander
Coriander seeds
Cumin
Fresh ginger
Garam masala
1 garlic clove
Ground fennel
Mint
Oregano
Parsley
Red chilli
Rosemary

Other:

Balsamic vinegar
Chicken stock
Chinese white wine vinegar
Cold pressed extra virgin olive oil
Corn flour
Dijon mustard
Fish stock
Peanut oil
Red wine vinegar
Sun dried tomatoes
Soy sauce
400g tinned tomatoes
Tomato puree
Vegetable stock
White wine vinegar

Snacks:

Fruit
Dr Karg crackers
Crackers/flat breads
Small bowl of muesli
Yoghurt/Alpro soya yoghurt
Nuts (cashew, pine or now and again mixed nuts)
Soya nuts
Seeds (pumpkin or sunflower)

Fruit drinks:

1 carton Tropicana/Innocent fruit drink

Shopping List
Week 5

Carbohydrates:

6 baked potatoes
1 bag of brown rice
260g of Jordans muesli
12 new potatoes
480g porridge oats
1 bag of rice noodles
1 bag of sunflower and pumpkin seeds
4 organic tortilla wraps
5 sweet potatoes
Wheat biscuits/Shredded wheat

Dairy and non-dairy alternatives:

8 eggs
150g greek yoghurt
50g parmesan cheese/goat's cheese
1760ml skimmed/Alpro soya/rice/oat milk
2.5kg Alpro soya yoghurt

Fish:

800g barramundi fillets
150g calamari
200g mussels
600g raw prawns
4 poached salmon fillets
4 tins tuna
400g white fish of your choice

Meat:

800g beef fillet
400g cooked roast beef
800g chicken on the bone
4 chicken breasts
1 large whole chicken
400g lean ham
800g boneless lamb

Fruit:

7 apples
2 apricots
9 bananas
1 punnet of blueberries
1 bag of green grapes
3 lemons
1 lime
2 peaches
1 punnet of raspberries

Vegetables:

16 asparagus
4 cooked beetroot
125g frozen broad beans
250g broccoli
250g cherry tomatoes
7 carrots
4 celery sticks
1 courgette
½ cucumber
3 lettuce
250g mange tout
175g mushrooms
4 onions
4 parsnips
50g frozen peas
175g runner beans
1 red onion
2 red peppers
16 red tomatoes
150g rocket salad
150g baby spinach
9 spring onions
150g sugar snap peas
1 turnip
1 yellow pepper

Herbs:

Basil
3 bay leaves
Black pepper
Coriander
Cumin
6 dill sprigs
1 fennel bulb
Fresh ginger
11 lemongrass stalks
1 garlic clove
Oregano
Paprika
Parsley
6 peppercorns
Red chilli
Rosemary
Saffron
Thyme

Other:

Balsamic vinegar
Chicken stock
Chinese white wine vinegar
Cold pressed extra virgin olive oil
Corn flour
Fish sauce
Prawn paste
Soy sauce
Sugar
800g tinned tomatoes
Tomato puree
Vegetable stock
Worcestershire sauce

Snacks:

Fruits
Dr Karg crackers
Crackers/flat breads
Small bowl of muesli
Yoghurt/Alpro soya yoghurt
Nuts (cashew, pine or occasionally mixed nuts)
Soya nuts
Seeds (pumpkin or sunflower)

Fruit drinks:

1 carton Tropicana/Innocent fruit

Shopping List
Week 6

Carbohydrates:

1 bag of black beans
1 bag of brown basmati rice
1 bag of brown rice
1 bag of wild rice
1 tin of chickpeas
1 bag of long grain rice
250g of Jordans muesli
320g porridge oats
1 bag of rice noodles
1 bag of sunflower seeds
1 bag of pumpkin seeds
4 organic tortilla wraps
1 bag of pine nuts
8 baked potatoes
4 sweet potatoes
4 organic tortilla wraps
225g water chestnuts
12 wholemeal/brown pitta breads
Wheat biscuits/Shredded wheat

Dairy and non-dairy alternatives:

200g feta/goat's cheese
50g goat's cheese
1.88 litres skimmed/Alpro soya/rice/oat milk
2kg Alpro soya yoghurt

Fish:

225g haddock fillets
225g smoked haddock fillets
700g cooked prawns
1.15kg tuna steaks
4 tinned tuna cans
225g x 4 white fish

Meat:

400g rump beef
8 chicken breasts
1 large whole chicken
400g lean ham
1.5kg leg of lamb
4 turkey breasts

Fruit:

7 apples
2 apricots
6 bananas
1 punnet of blackberries
1 punnet of blueberries
4 lemons
4 peaches
1 large pineapple
1 punnet of raspberries

Vegetables:

115g baby corn
300g baby spinach
4 cooked beetroot
12 black olives
225g broccoli
1.4kg butternut squash
6 cherry tomatoes
4 carrots
4 celery sticks
1 cos lettuce
1 courgette
1½ cucumber
2 leeks
2 lettuce
50g mange tout
3 onions
8 plum tomatoes
2 red onions
2 red peppers
4 red tomatoes
175g rocket salad
4 shallots
20 spring onions
1 turnip
1 yellow pepper

Herbs:

Basil
Black pepper
Chilli powder
Coriander
Ground coriander
Coriander seeds
Fresh ginger
2 green chillies
1 garlic clove
Mint
Nutmeg
Paprika
Parsley
4 red chillies
Rosemary
Turmeric

Other:

Balsamic vinegar
Brown sugar
150ml coconut milk
Chicken stock
Chinese rice vinegar
Cold pressed extra virgin olive oil
Peanut oil
Soy sauce
Tahini
400g tinned tomatoes
Vegetable stock
115ml white wine

Snacks:

Fruit
Dr Karg crackers
Crackers/flat breads
Small bowl of muesli
Yoghurt/Alpro soya yoghurt
Nuts (cashew, pine or occasionally mixed nuts)
Soya nuts
Seeds (pumpkin or sunflower)

Fruit drinks:

1 carton Tropicana/Innocent fruit drink

Shopping List
Week 7

Carbohydrates:

1 bag of brown rice
12 charlotte potatoes
240g of Jordans muesli
560g porridge oats
1 bag of rice noodles
1 bag of sunflower
1 bag of pumpkin seeds
4 organic tortilla wraps
1 bag of sesame seeds
5 sweet potatoes
4 wholemeal/brown pitta breads
225g yellow split peas
Wheat biscuits/Shredded wheat

Dairy and non-dairy alternatives:

12 eggs
60g feta/goat's cheese
680ml skimmed/Alpro soya/rice/
oat milk
2kg Alpro soya yoghurt

Fish:

200g x 4 barramundi
175g x 4 cod/hake
200g x 4 snapper fillets
4 poached salmon fillets
4 tins tuna

Meat:

400g cooked roast beef
12 chicken breasts
400g lean ham
1.4kg lamb cutlets

Fruit:

3 apples
4 bananas
2 lemons
2 limes
2 mangos
1 melon
1 orange
1 large pineapple
1 punnet of raspberries

Vegetables:

100g baby corn
3 bags of baby spinach
55g button mushrooms
1 broccoli floret
350g cabbage
400g cherry tomatoes
3 carrots
1 courgette
1½ cucumbers
2 fennel bulbs
1 green pepper
4 lettuce
200g mange tout
150g mushrooms
5 onions
5 red onions
4 red peppers
100g rocket salad
200g savoy cabbage
230g snow pea pods
11 spring onions
5 yellow peppers

Herbs:

Basil
Black pepper
Cardamom seeds
Chilli powder
Chinese five spice
Cinnamon
Coriander
Cumin
Fresh ginger
1 garlic clove
Mint
Oregano
Parsley
1 red chilli
Rosemary
Tarragon

Other:

Balsamic vinegar
Cider vinegar
Cold pressed extra virgin olive oil
Dijon mustard
Oyster stock
Peanut oil
Sesame oil
Soy sauce
Tomato puree
Vegetable stock
60ml white wine

Snacks:

Fruits:
Dr Karg crackers
Crackers/flat breads
Small bowl of muesli
Yoghurt/Alpro soya yoghurt
Nuts (cashew, pine or occasionally mixed nuts)
Soya nuts
Seeds (pumpkin or sunflower)

Fruit drinks:

1 carton Tropicana/Innocent fruit drink

Shopping List
Week 8

Carbohydrates:

80g almonds
1 bag of brown rice
1 bag of couscous
400g kidney beans
240g of Jordans muesli
1 bag of pine nuts
125g new potatoes
400g pinto beans
560g porridge oats
12 potatoes
1 bag of sunflower seeds
1 bag of pumpkin seeds
8 sweet potatoes
8 wholemeal/brown pitta breads
Wheat biscuits/Shredded wheat

Dairy and non-dairy alternatives:

20 eggs
20g feta/goat's cheese
50g soft goat's/low fat
   cream cheese
880ml skimmed/Alpro soya/rice/oat milk
1.7kg Alpro soya yoghurt

Fish:

8 anchovy fillets
4 cooked mackerel
225g fresh mackerel
800g cooked prawns
4 salmon fillets
1 pack smoked salmon (for 4)
1.15kg tuna steaks
4 tins tuna

Meat:

1lb lean minced beef
400g roast beef
8 chicken breasts
400g lean ham
800g leg of lamb

Fruit:

4 apples
1 apricot
8 bananas
1 punnet of blackberries
1 punnet of blueberries
3 lemons
2 limes
2 mangos
1 melon
2 oranges
1 peach
1 large pineapple
1 punnet of raspberries

Vegetables:

2 avocados
600g baby spinach
25g black olives
75g broccoli
250g cherry tomatoes
3 carrots
3 celery sticks
2 courgettes
½ cucumber
175g french beans
2 leeks
3 lettuce
8 large mushrooms
50g mange tout
5 onions
2 parsnips
115g plum tomatoes
3 red onions
4 red peppers
23 tomatoes
100g rocket salad
1 shallot
10 spring onions

Herbs:

Basil
2 bay leaves
Black pepper
Chives
Coriander
Cumin
Fresh ginger
1 garlic clove
Parsley
2 red chillies
Rosemary

Other:

Balsamic vinegar
Chicken stock
Chinese white rice vinegar
Cold pressed extra virgin olive oil
Corn flour
Dijon mustard
Light soy sauce
Peanut oil
60ml red wine
Soy sauce
Sugar
400g tinned tomatoes
Tomato puree
Whole grain mustard

Snacks:

Fruit
Dr Karg crackers
Crackers/flat breads
Small bowl of muesli
Yoghurt/Alpro soya yoghurt
Nuts (cashew, pine or now and again mixed nuts)
Soya nuts
Seeds (pumpkin or sunflower)

Fruit drinks:

1 carton Tropicana/Innocent fruit drink

Shopping List
Week 9

Carbohydrates:

1 bag of brown rice
1 bag of couscous
260g of Jordans muesli
560g porridge oats
12 potatoes
1 bag of sunflower seeds
1 bag of pumpkin seeds
5 sweet potatoes
4 wholemeal/brown pitta breads
225g yellow split peas
1 bag of wild rice
Wheat biscuits/Shredded wheat

Dairy and non-dairy alternatives:

12 eggs
2105ml skimmed/Alpro soya/rice/oat milk
2kg Alpro soya yoghurt

Fish:

6 anchovy fillets
4 monkfish tails
225g raw peeled prawns
4 poached salmon fillets
200g x 4 salmon steaks
4 tins tuna
450g white fish of your choice

Meat:

800g rump beef steak
8 chicken breasts
400g lean ham
400g turkey breast

Fruit:

8 apples
2 apricots
6 bananas
1 punnet of blackberries
1 punnet of blueberries
4 lemons
2 limes
1 melon
2 oranges
2 peaches
1 large pineapple
1 punnet of raspberries

Vegetables:

16 asparagus spears
1 avocado
1 baby gem lettuce
350g baby spinach
150g bean sprouts
4 cooked beetroots
1.4kg butternut squash
650g cherry tomatoes
5 carrots
2 celery sticks
1 courgette
1½ cucumber
3 lettuce
50g mange tout
4 onions
115g plum tomatoes
3 red onions
4 red peppers
5 red tomatoes
100g rocket salad
5 shallots
11 spring onions
5 yellow peppers

Herbs:

Chilli powder
Chives
Coriander
Ground coriander
Cumin
Curry powder
Fresh ginger
1 garlic clove
1 green chilli
Mint
Nutmeg
Paprika
Parsley
1 red chilli
Rosemary
Turmeric

Other:

Balsamic vinegar
Chicken stock
Cider vinegar
150ml coconut milk
Cold pressed extra virgin olive oil
Corn flour
Dijon mustard
Fish sauce
Honey
115ml lemon juice
Soy sauce
Tomato puree
Vegetable stock
Worchester sauce

Snacks:

Fruit
Dr Karg crackers
Crackers/flat breads
Small bowl of muesli
Yoghurt/Alpro soya yoghurt
Nuts (cashew, pine or occasionally mixed nuts)
Soya nuts
Seeds (pumpkin or sunflower)

Fruit drinks:

1 carton Tropicana/Innocent fruit drink

Shopping List
Week 10

Carbohydrates:

1 bag of brown rice
1 bag of couscous
240g of Jordans muesli
560g porridge oats
4 potatoes
1 bag of sunflower seeds
1 bag of pumpkin seeds
4 sweet potatoes
4 organic tortilla wraps
4 wholemeal/brown pitta breads
1 bag of wild rice
Wheat biscuits/Shredded wheat

Dairy and non-dairy alternatives:

8 eggs
200g ricotta cheese/goat's cheese
680ml skimmed/Alpro soya/rice/oat milk
1.5kg Alpro soya yoghurt

Fish:

8 anchovy fillets
350g cod or haddock
4 marlin steaks
350g monkfish
16 large raw prawns
200g x 4 swordfish steaks
4 tins tuna

Meat:

400g cooked roast beef
8 chicken breasts
400g lean ham
350g boneless lamb
800g rack of lamb
4 turkey breasts

Fruit:

6 apples
1 apricot
8 bananas
1 punnet of blackberries
4 lemons
2 limes
2 mangos
2 oranges
1 peach
1 large pineapple
1 punnet of raspberries
1 watermelon

Vegetables:

2 aubergines
200g baby carrots
4 cooked beetroots
1kg butternut squash
24 black olives
4 carrots
8 celery sticks
8 courgettes
1 cucumber
75g french beans
200g green beans
1 green pepper
2 lettuce
50g mange tout
6 onions
200g peas
150g plum tomatoes
4 red onions
4 red peppers
14 red tomatoes
100g rocket salad
4 shaliots
10 spring onions
2 yellow peppers

Herbs:

Basil
Black pepper
Chilli powder
Chives
Cinnamon sticks
Ground coriander
Cumin
Fresh ginger
1 garlic clove
1 green chilli
Mint
Nutmeg
Oregano
Paprika
Parsley
Rosemary
Tarragon
Thyme sprigs
Turmeric

Other:

175g dried apricots
Balsamic vinegar
Chicken stock
Chinese rice vinegar
Cold pressed extra virgin olive oil
Dijon mustard
Fish stock
Honey
Light soy sauce
Plain flour
60ml red wine
Soy sauce
Sugar
Tabasco sauce
400g tinned tomatoes
Tomato puree
Vegetable stock

Snacks:

Fruit
Dr Karg crackers
Crackers/flat breads
Small bowl of muesli
Yoghurt/Alpro soya yoghurt
Nuts (cashew, pine or occasionally mixed nuts)
Soya nuts
Seeds (pumpkin or sunflower)

Fruit drinks:

1 carton Tropicana/Innocent fruit drink

Shopping List
Week 11

Carbohydrates:

1 bag of brown rice
1 bag of couscous
240g of Jordans muesli
560g porridge oats
4 potatoes
1 bag of sunflower seeds
1 bag of pumpkin seeds
4 sweet potatoes
4 organic tortilla wraps
4 wholemeal/brown pitta breads
1 bag of wild rice
Wheat biscuits/Shredded wheat

Dairy and non-dairy alternatives:

8 eggs
200g ricotta/goat's cheese
680ml skimmed/Alpro soya/rice/oat milk
1.5kg Alpro soya yoghurt

Fish:

8 anchovy fillets
350g cod or haddock
4 marlin steaks
350g monkfish
16 large raw prawns
200g x 4 swordfish steaks
4 tins tuna

Meat:

400g cooked roast beef
8 chicken breasts
400g lean ham
350g boneless lamb
800g rack of lamb
4 turkey breasts

Fruit:

6 apples
1 apricot
8 bananas
1 punnet of blackberries
4 lemons
2 limes
2 mangos
2 oranges
1 peach
1 large pineapple
1 punnet of raspberries
1 watermelon

Vegetables:

2 aubergines
200g baby carrots
4 cooked beetroots
1kg butternut squash
24 black olives
4 carrots
8 celery sticks
8 courgettes
1 cucumber
75g french beans
200g green beans
1 green pepper
2 lettuce
50g mange tout
6 onions
200g peas
150g plum tomatoes
4 red onions
4 red peppers
14 red tomatoes
100g rocket salad
4 shallots
10 spring onions
2 yellow peppers

Herbs:

Basil
Black pepper
Chilli powder
Chives
Cinnamon sticks
Ground coriander
Cumin
Fresh ginger
1 garlic clove
1 green chilli
Mint
Nutmeg
Oregano
Paprika
Parsley
Rosemary
Tarragon
Thyme sprigs
Turmeric

Other:

175g dried apricots
Balsamic vinegar
Chicken stock
Chinese rice vinegar
Cold pressed extra virgin olive oil
Dijon mustard
Fish stock
Honey
Light soy sauce
Plain flour
60ml red wine
Soy sauce
Sugar
Tabasco sauce
400g tinned tomatoes
Tomato puree
Vegetable stock

Snacks:

Fruit
Dr Karg crackers
Crackers/flat breads
Small bowl of muesli
Yoghurt/Alpro soya yoghurt
Nuts (cashew, pine or occasionally mixed nuts)
Soya nuts
Seeds (pumpkin or sunflower)

Fruit drinks:

1 carton Tropicana/Innocent fruit

Shopping List
Week 12

Carbohydrates:

75g brown basmati rice
50g wholegrain brown barley
1 bag of brown rice
400g kidney beans
225g lentils
25g millet seeds
250g of Jordans muesli
125g new potatoes
1 bag of pine nuts
400g pinto beans
560g porridge oats
3 potatoes
1 bag of sunflower seeds
1 bag pumpkin seeds
12 sweet potatoes
8 wholemeal or brown pitta breads
Wheat biscuits/Shredded wheat

Dairy and non-dairy alternatives:

8 eggs
60g feta/goat's cheese
1880ml skimmed/Alpro soya/rice/oat milk
1.7kg Alpro soya soghurt

Fish:

8 anchovy fillets
225g fresh mackerel
600g monkfish tail
4 salmon fillets
8 king size prawns
4 rainbow trout
4 sea bass fillets
4 pack of smoked salmon
4 small tins tuna
350g tuna steaks

Meat:

8 chicken breasts
8 chicken thighs
100g raw chorizo
100g raw garlic sausage
2kg lamb shank
400g lean ham

Fruit:

8 apples
2 apricots
10 bananas
1 lime
3 lemons
1 mango
2 oranges
2 peaches
1 large pineapple
1 small packet of raisins
1 punnet of raspberries
1 watermelon

Vegetables:

3 avocados
100g baby corn
2 bags of baby spinach
1.4kg butternut squash
25g black olives
250g cherry tomatoes
5 carrots
4 celery sticks
3 courgettes
½ cucumber
175g french beans
2 green peppers
2 lettuces
50g mange tout
1 marrow
150g mushrooms
6 onions
115g plum tomatoes
1 red onion
5 red peppers
8 red tomatoes
100g rocket salad
1 shallot
100g sugar snap peas
10 spring onions
2 yellow peppers

Herbs:

Basil
2 bay leaves
Black pepper
Coriander
Ground coriander
Ground cumin
Dill
1 garlic clove
Fresh ginger
1 lemongrass stalk
Nutmeg
Oregano
Paprika
Parsley
2 red chillies
Rosemary
Thyme
Turmeric

Other:

Balsamic vinegar
Chicken stock
400ml coconut milk
Cold pressed extra virgin olive oil
Dijon mustard
Plain flour
400g tinned plum tomatoes
vegetable stock
115ml white wine
White wine vinegar

Snacks:

Fruit
Dr Karg crackers
Crackers/flat breads
Small bowl of muesli
Yoghurt/Alpro soya yoghurt
Nuts (cashew, pine or occasionally mixed nuts)
Soya nuts
Seeds (pumpkin or sunflower)

Fruit drinks:

1 carton Tropicana/Innocent fruit

Your Next Steps

This 12-week Nutrition Programme book is just one part of the Train to Become series. In order to get the maximum results from your 12-week programme, use this book in conjunction with the Train to Become Fitness and General Health Guide to do the Train to Become Challenge. These books clearly show that with commitment and determination, you really can achieve a healthier and happier you!

If you need a little extra support or would like some additional advice, please visit my website at **www.traintobecome.com** and feel free to contact me by email at **contact@traintobecome.com**.

Train to Become Challenge

Train to Become Fitness is part of a three book collection dedicated to showing you how to change your body and lifestyle in just 12 weeks. All three books have been put together to exactly show how you can change your body and lifestyle in just 12 weeks for the better.

Train to Become – General Health Guide

This is based on your lifestyle. It looks at your body and posture, your skin and what is the best thing to do to counteract certain skin and body conditions.

We look at a daily guide as to how my body changed following this 12-week plan and how eventually your body can change for the better too.

Train to Become – 12-week Fitness Programme

Shows you in great detail the exercises and fitness programmes for you to follow that will help you to get into amazing shape and build your muscles and fitness over a 12 week period and beyond.

Follow my own fitness diary as a guide and create your own.

Train to Become – 12-week Fitness Programme

Shows you in great detail the exercises and fitness programmes for you to follow to help you get into amazing shape, by losing weight, toning up and getting fitter in just 12-weeks.

Follow the fitness diary as a guide to create your veryown diary that is provided for you.

Train to Become – 12-week Nutrition Programme

Focuses on exactly what I ate following the 12-week plan, it also shows when I ate and how often too. It guides you through every day with recipes for breakfast, lunch and dinner.

It also has a weekly shopping list and snack list to help you along your way. I found keeping a personal diary very useful to show any food patterns and to monitor my treats!

Don't just take my word for it. You can see the results for yourself in the pictures in all the books throughout the series.

Useful contacts

Train to Become
For all Train to Become books, up and coming events on training and locations for Train to Become personal trainers please visit: **www.traintobecome.com**

Myo Clinic
Home to the Myo Massage treatments and special health and medical packages please visit: **www.myoclinic.co.uk**

Hay Outdoor Training
For all forthcoming Train to Become events, as well as outdoor training details, please visit: **www.training-activities.co.uk**

Alpro, Jordans and Innocent Drinks
We would like to thank you for your help and support with our book launch. We found your products and service exceptional.

Index